BOB DYLAN

FOR CLAWHAMMER BANJO

Arranged by Michael Miles

ISBN 978-1-4803-6406-6

Music Sales America

EXCLUSIVELY DISTRIBUTED BY

HAL•LEONARD®
CORPORATION

7777 W. BLUEMOUND RD. P.O. BOX 13819 MILWAUKEE, WI 53213

Visit Hal Leonard Online at
www.halleonard.com

CONTENTS

G TUNING

DOUBLE C TUNING

D TUNING

D MINOR TUNING

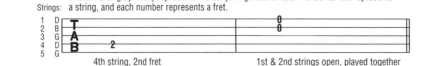

BANJO NOTATION LEGEND

TABLATURE graphically represents the banjo fingerboard. Each horizontal line represents a string, and each number represents a fret.

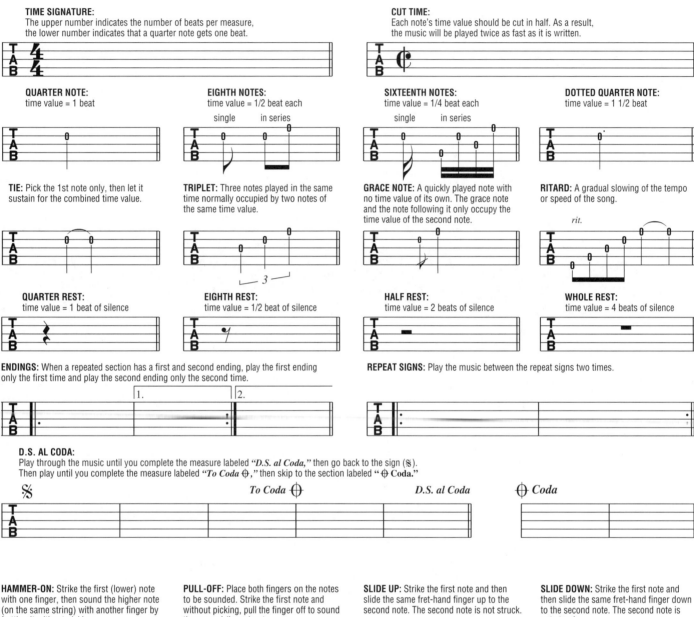

TIME SIGNATURE: The upper number indicates the number of beats per measure, the lower number indicates that a quarter note gets one beat.

CUT TIME: Each note's time value should be cut in half. As a result, the music will be played twice as fast as it is written.

QUARTER NOTE: time value = 1 beat

EIGHTH NOTES: time value = 1/2 beat each
single   in series

SIXTEENTH NOTES: time value = 1/4 beat each
single   in series

DOTTED QUARTER NOTE: time value = 1 1/2 beat

TIE: Pick the 1st note only, then let it sustain for the combined time value.

TRIPLET: Three notes played in the same time normally occupied by two notes of the same time value.

GRACE NOTE: A quickly played note with no time value of its own. The grace note and the note following it only occupy the time value of the second note.

RITARD: A gradual slowing of the tempo or speed of the song.

QUARTER REST: time value = 1 beat of silence

EIGHTH REST: time value = 1/2 beat of silence

HALF REST: time value = 2 beats of silence

WHOLE REST: time value = 4 beats of silence

ENDINGS: When a repeated section has a first and second ending, play the first ending only the first time and play the second ending only the second time.

REPEAT SIGNS: Play the music between the repeat signs two times.

D.S. AL CODA:
Play through the music until you complete the measure labeled *"D.S. al Coda,"* then go back to the sign (%).
Then play until you complete the measure labeled *"To Coda ⊕,"* then skip to the section labeled "⊕ **Coda.**"

To Coda ⊕   *D.S. al Coda*   ⊕ *Coda*

HAMMER-ON: Strike the first (lower) note with one finger, then sound the higher note (on the same string) with another finger by fretting it without picking.

PULL-OFF: Place both fingers on the notes to be sounded. Strike the first note and without picking, pull the finger off to sound the second (lower) note.

SLIDE UP: Strike the first note and then slide the same fret-hand finger up to the second note. The second note is not struck.

SLIDE DOWN: Strike the first note and then slide the same fret-hand finger down to the second note. The second note is not struck.

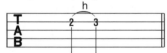  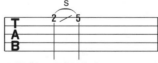 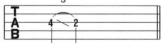

HALF-STEP CHOKE: Strike the note and bend the string up 1/2 step.

WHOLE-STEP CHOKE: Strike the note and bend the string up one step.

NATURAL HARMONIC: Strike the note while the fret-hand lightly touches the string directly over the fret indicated.

BRUSH: Play the notes of the chord indicated by quickly rolling them from bottom to top.

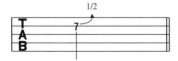   

Scruggs/Keith Tuners:

HALF-TWIST UP: Strike the note, twist tuner up 1/2 step, and continue playing.

HALF-TWIST DOWN: Strike the note, twist tuner down 1/2 step, and continue playing.

WHOLE-TWIST UP: Strike the note, twist tuner up one step, and continue playing.

WHOLE-TWIST DOWN: Strike the note, twist tuner down one step, and continue playing.

 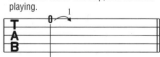

Right Hand Fingerings

t = thumb   i = index finger   m = middle finger

All Along the Watchtower

Words and Music by Bob Dylan

D Minor tuning:
(5th-1st) A-D-F-A-D

Key of D minor

Intro
Moderately fast

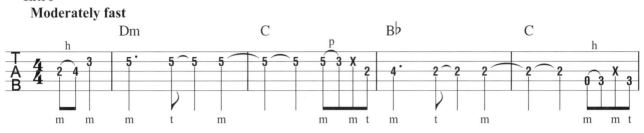

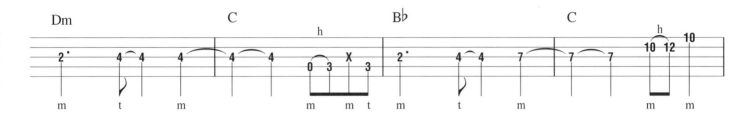

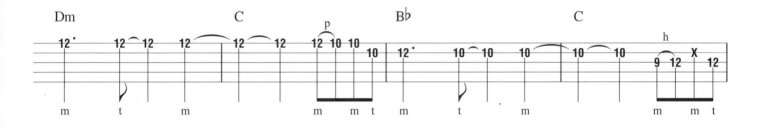

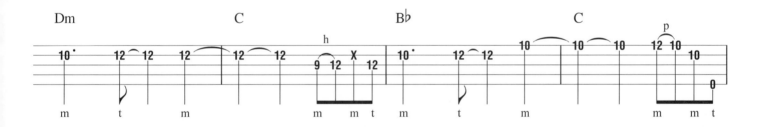

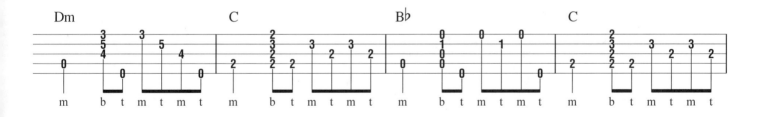

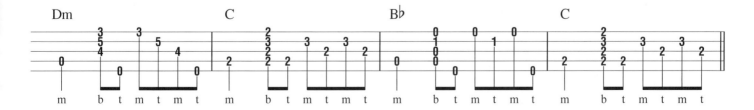

5

Verse

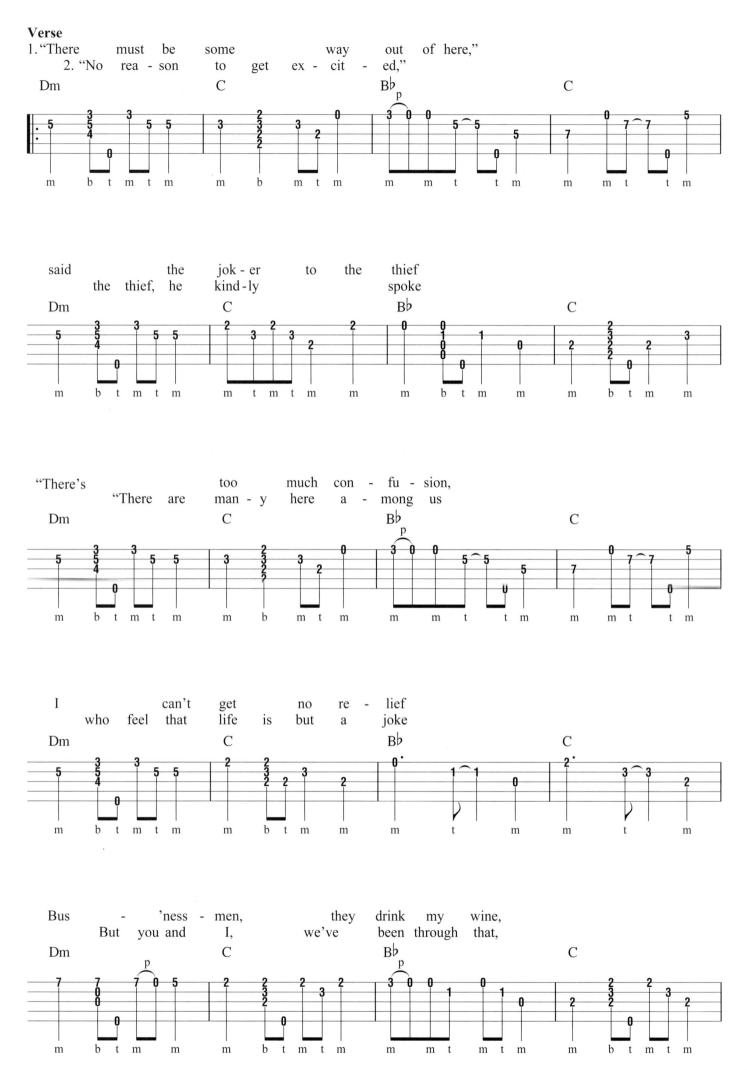

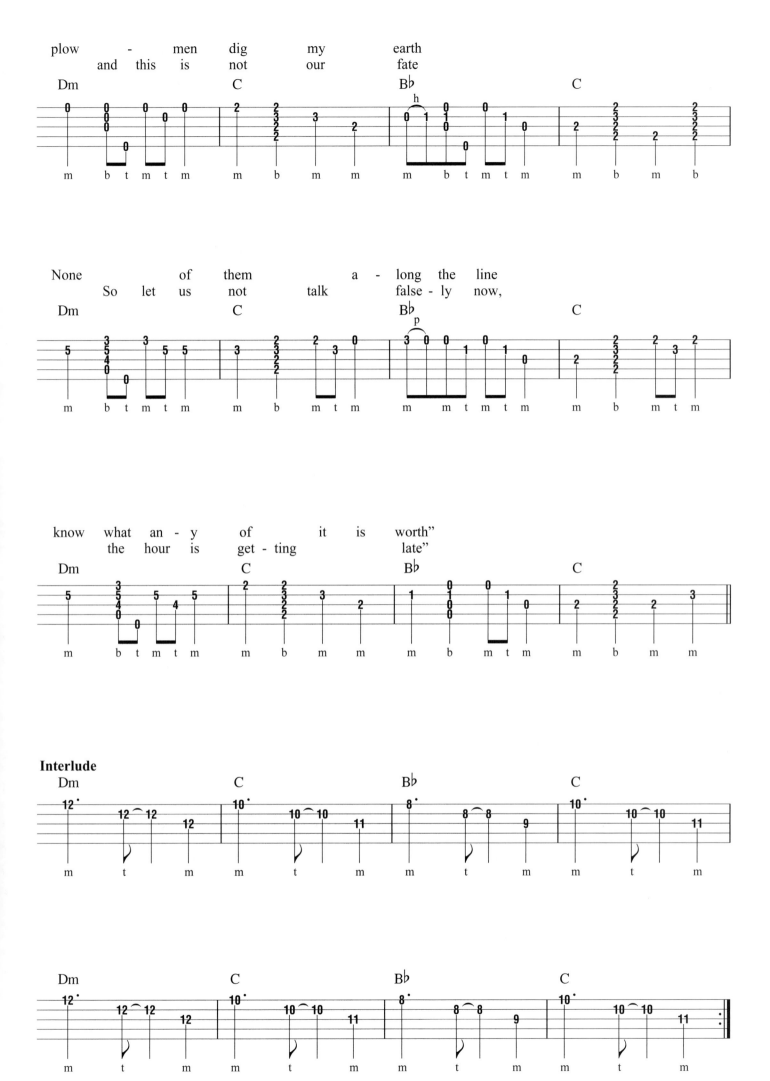

Chorus

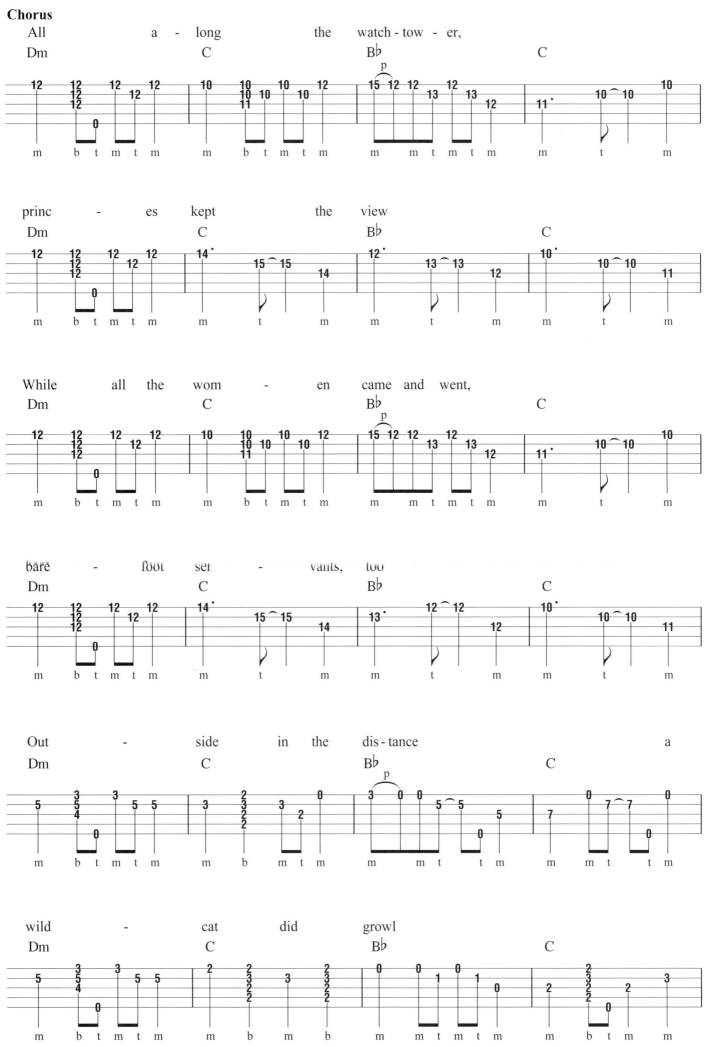

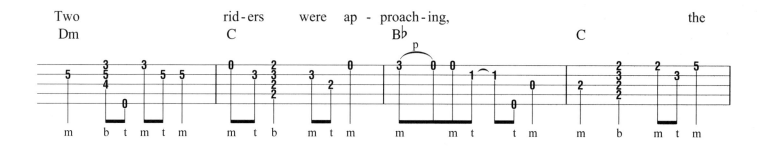

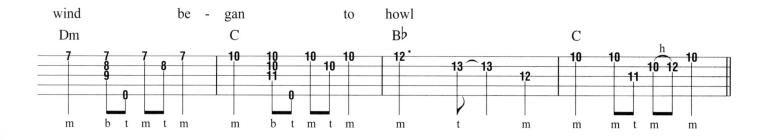

Outro

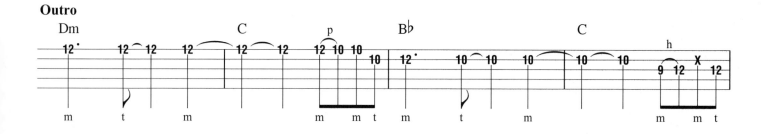

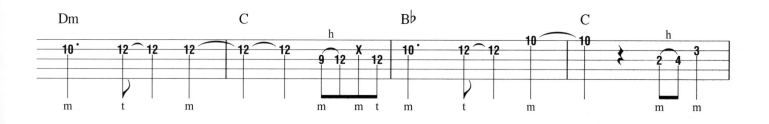

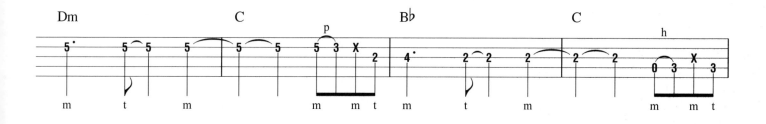

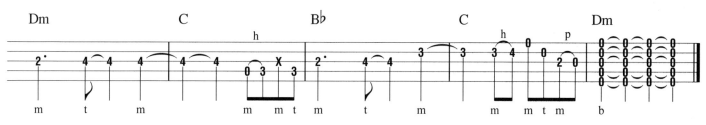

Blowin' in the Wind

Words and Music by Bob Dylan

G tuning:
(5th-1st) G-D-G-B-D

Key of G

Moderately slow

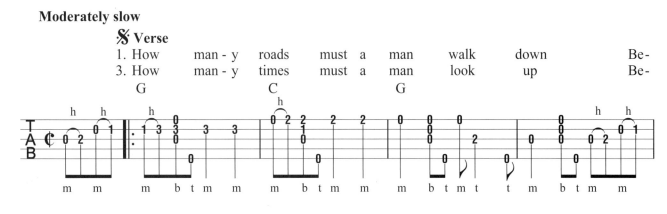

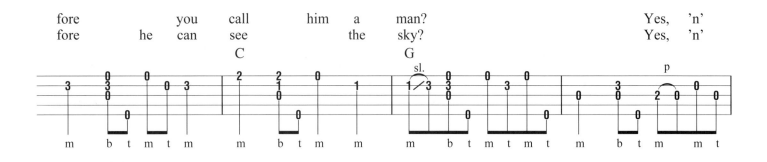

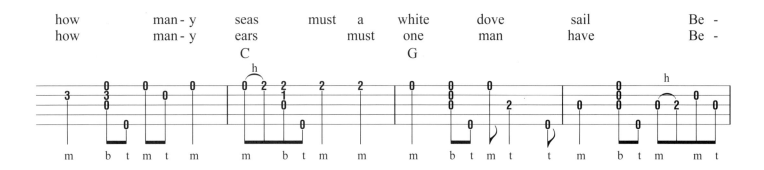

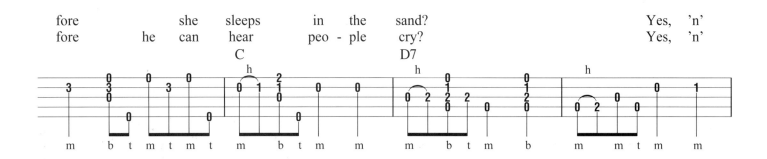

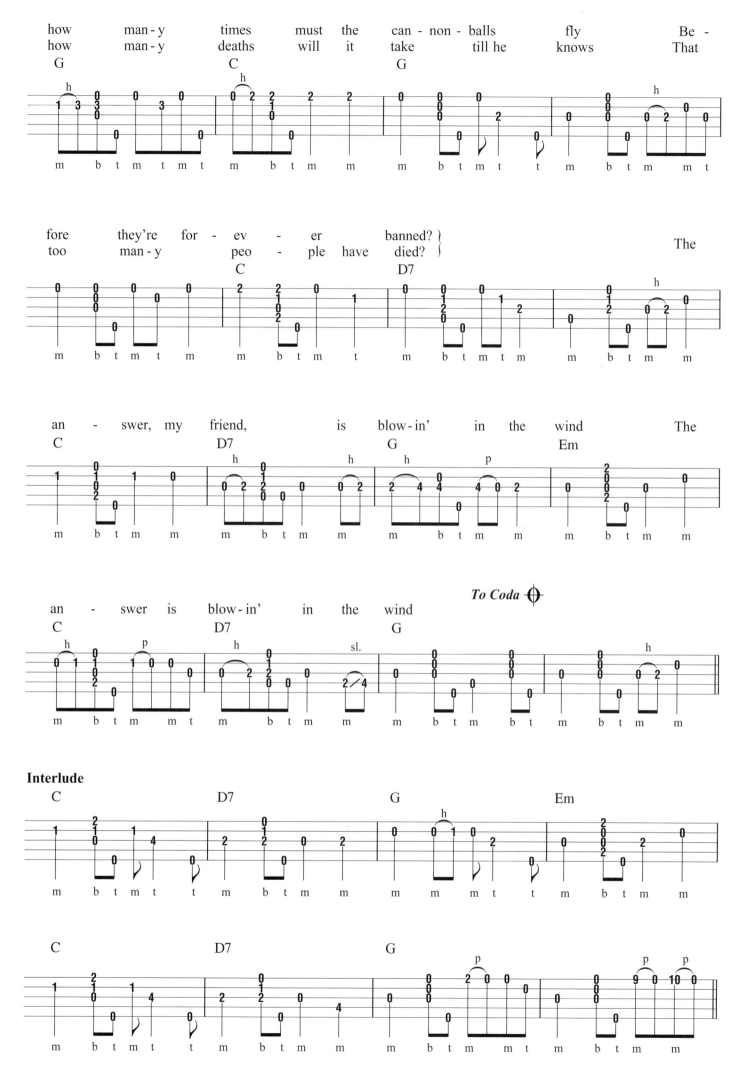

Verse

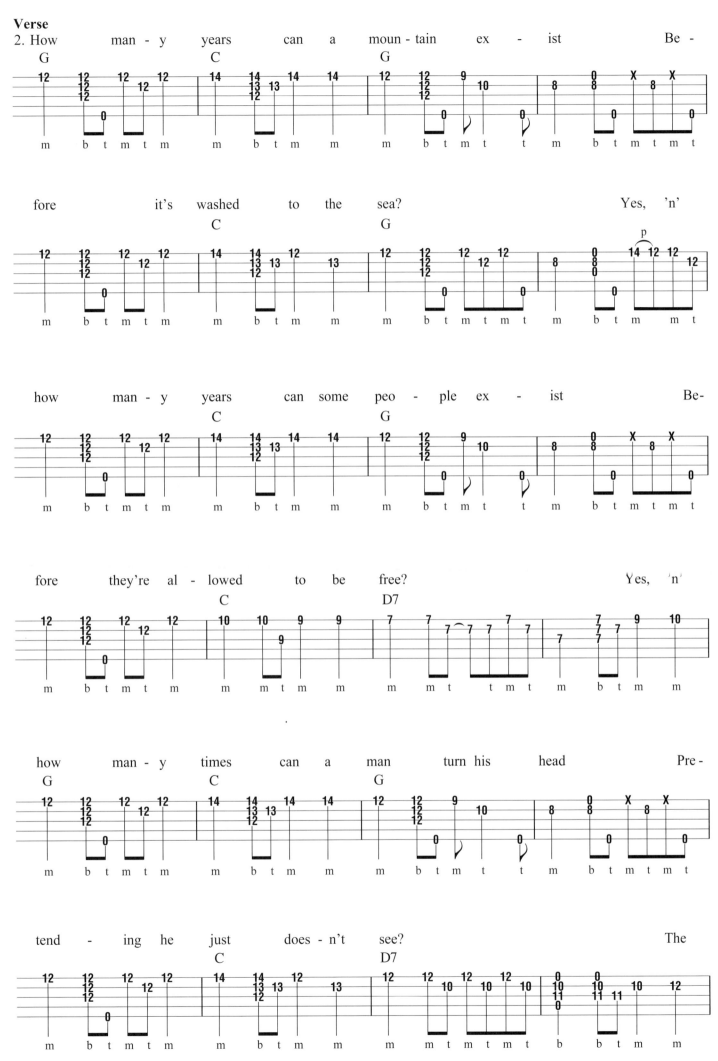

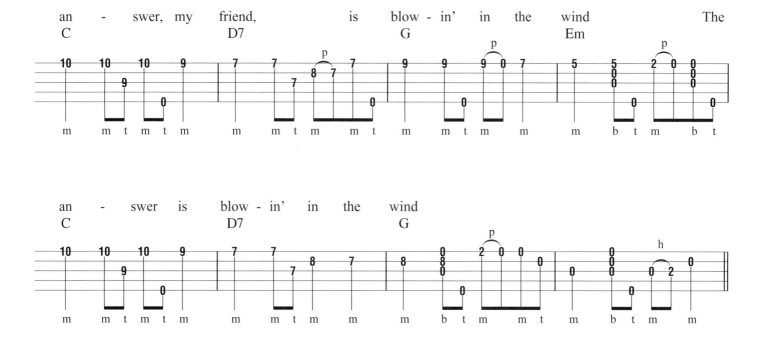

an - swer, my friend, is blow - in' in the wind The

an - swer is blow - in' in the wind

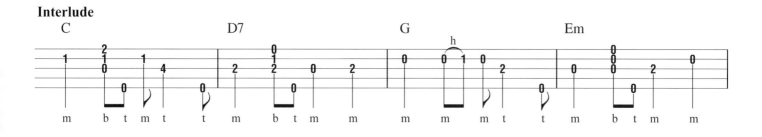

Interlude

D.S. al Coda

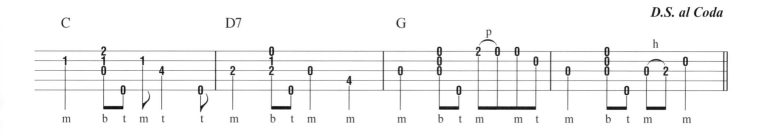

Coda

Outro

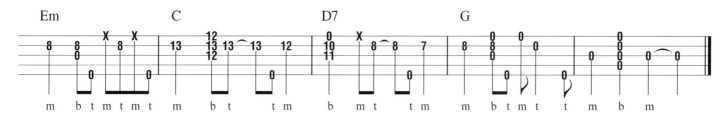

Don't Think Twice, It's All Right

Words and Music by Bob Dylan

Double C tuning:
(5th–1st) G-C-G-C-D

Key of C

Intro
  Moderately

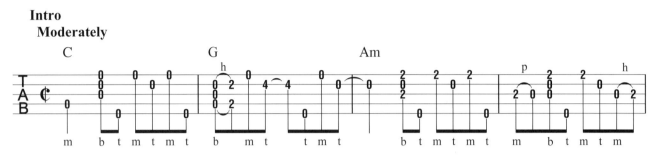

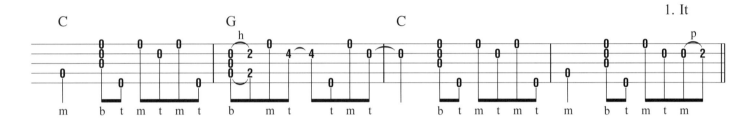

1. It

Verse

ain't no use to sit and won-der why, babe
2.–4., *See additional lyrics*

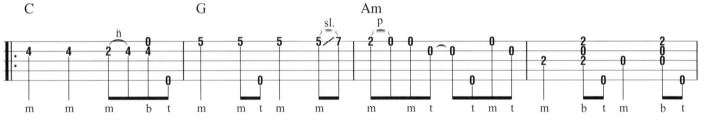

It don't mat-ter, any-how   An' it

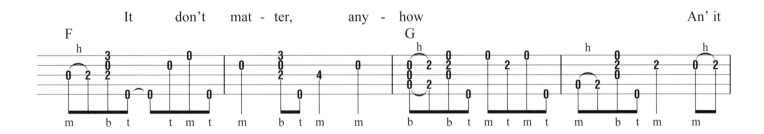

ain't no use to sit and won-der why, babe

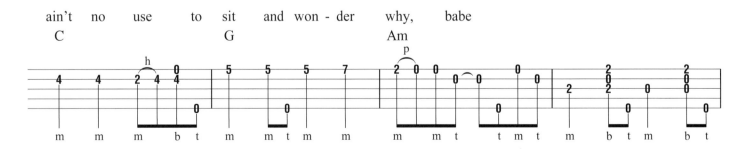

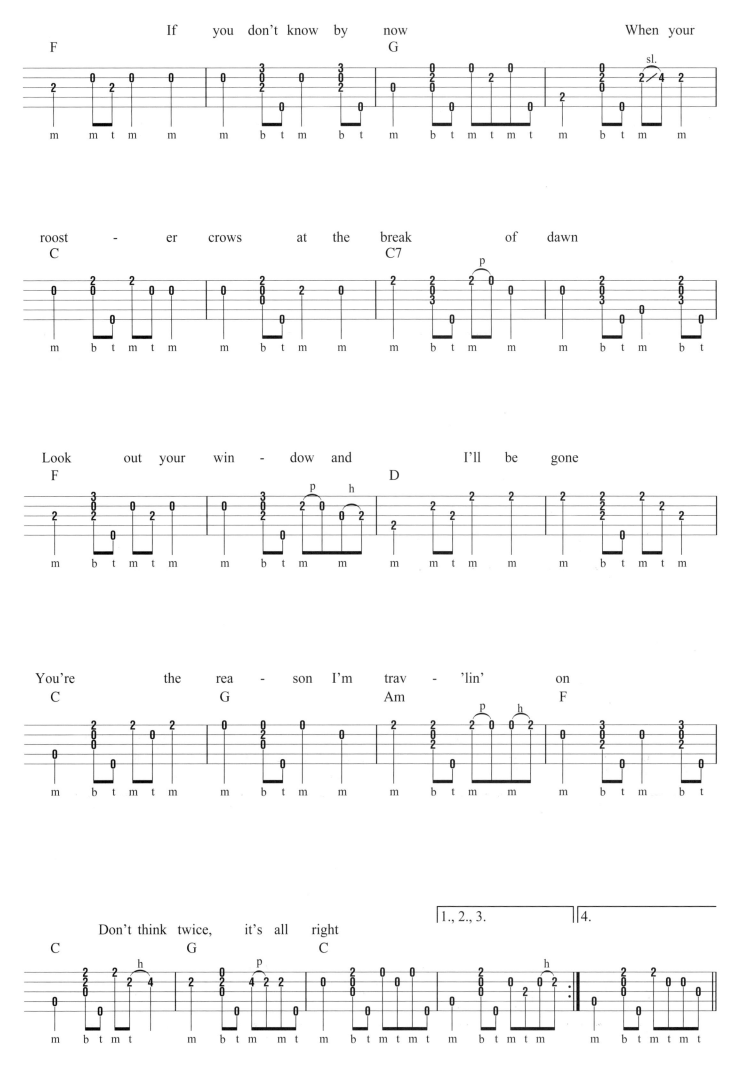

Banjo Break

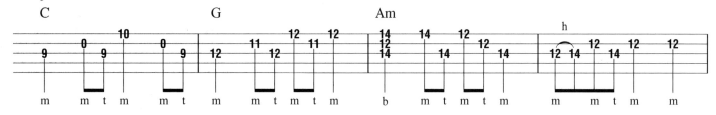

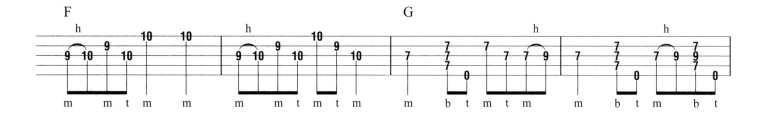

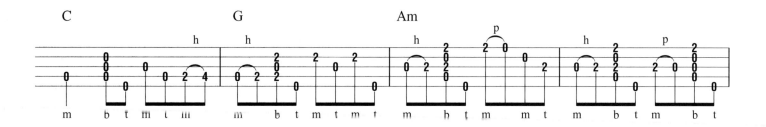

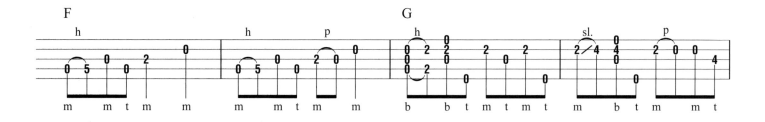

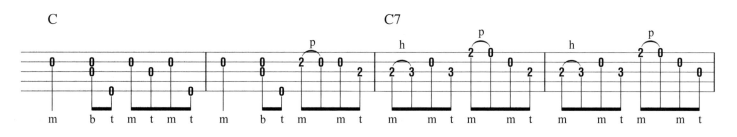

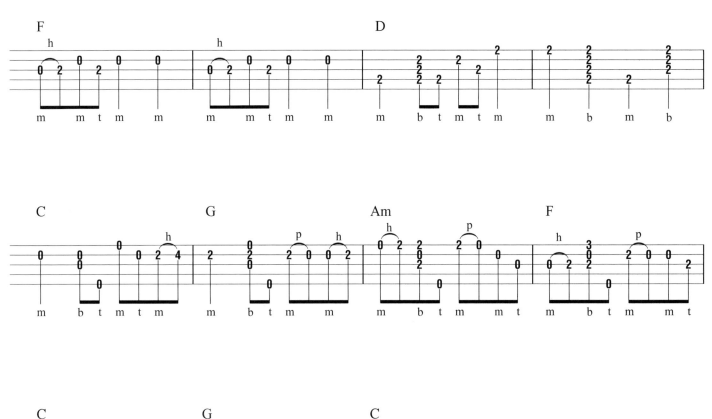

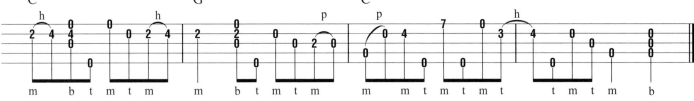

Additional Lyrics

2. It ain't no use in turnin' on your light, babe
   That light I never knowed
   An' it ain't no use in turnin' on your light, babe
   I'm on the dark side of the road
   Still I wish there was somethin' you would do or say
   To try and make me change my mind and stay
   We never did too much talkin' anyway
   So don't think twice, it's all right

3. It ain't no use in callin' out my name, gal
   Like you never did before
   It ain't no use in callin' out my name, gal
   I can't hear you anymore
   I'm a-thinkin' and a-wond'rin' all the way down the road
   I once loved a woman, a child I'm told
   I give her my heart but she wanted my soul
   But don't think twice, it's all right

4. I'm walkin' down that long, lonesome road, babe
   Where I'm bound, I can't tell
   But goodbye's too good a word, gal
   So I'll just say fare thee well
   I ain't sayin' you treated me unkind
   You could have done better but I don't mind
   You just kinda wasted my precious time
   But don't think twice, it's all right

Hurricane

Words and Music by Bob Dylan and Jacques Levy

D Minor tuning:
(5th-1st) A-D-F-A-D

Key of F

Intro/Interlude
Moderately

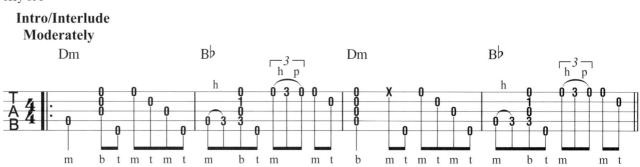

Verse

1. Pis - tol shots ring out in the bar - room night   En - ter Pat - ty Val - en - tine from
2.–11. *See additional lyrics*

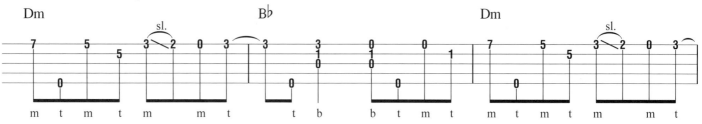

the up - per hall   She sees the bar - ten - der in   a pool of blood

Cries out, "My God, they killed them all!"   Here comes the sto - ry of the

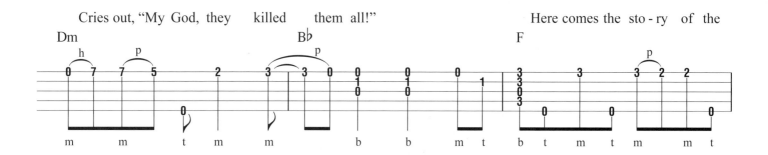

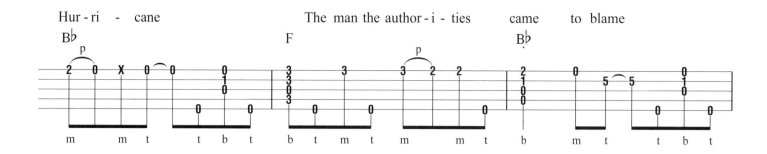

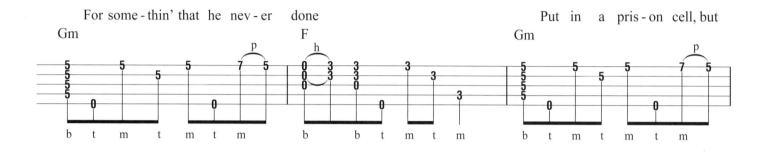

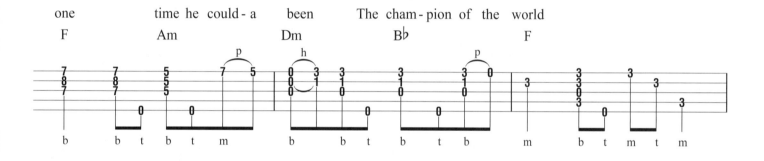

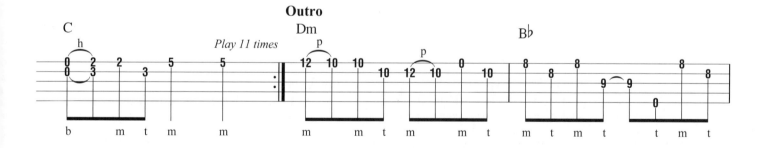

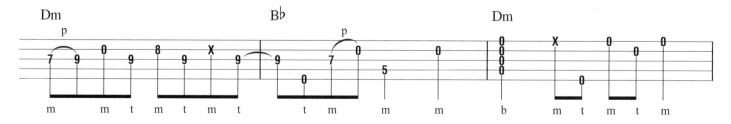

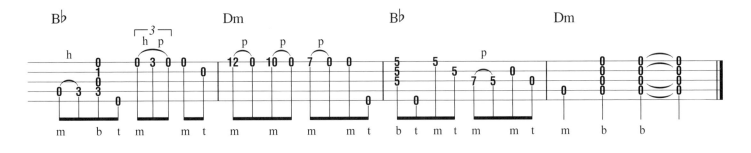

Additional Lyrics

2. Three bodies lyin' there does Patty see
And another man named Bello, movin' around mysteriously
"I didn't do it," he says, and he throws up his hands
"I was only robbin' the register, I hope you understand
I saw them leavin'," he says, and he stops
"One of us had better call up the cops"
And so Patty calls the cops
And they arrive on the scene with their red lights flashin'
In the hot New Jersey night

3. Meanwhile, far away in another part of town
Rubin Carter and a couple of friends are drivin' around
Number one contender for the middleweight crown
Had no idea what kinda shit was about to go down
When a cop pulled him over to the side of the road
Just like the time before and the time before that
In Paterson that's just the way things go
If you're black you might as well not show up on the street
'Less you wanna draw the heat

4. Alfred Bello had a partner and he had a rap for the cops
Him and Arthur Dexter Bradley were just out prowlin' around
He said, "I saw two men runnin' out, they looked like middleweights
They jumped into a white car with out-of-state plates"
And Miss Patty Valentine just nodded her head
Cop said, "Wait a minute, boys, this one's not dead"
So they took him to the infirmary
And though this man could hardly see
They told him that he could identify the guilty men

5. Four in the mornin' and they haul Rubin in
Take him to the hospital and they bring him upstairs
The wounded man looks up through his one dyin' eye
Says, "Wha'd you bring him in here for? He ain't the guy!"
Yes, here's the story of the Hurricane
The man the authorities came to blame
For somethin' that he never done
Put in a prison cell, but one time he could-a been
The champion of the world

6. Four months later, the ghettos are in flame
Rubin's in South America, fightin' for his name
While Arthur Dexter Bradley's still in the robbery game
And the cops are puttin' the screws to him, lookin' for somebody to blame
"Remember that murder that happened in a bar?"
"Remember you said you saw the getaway car?"
"You think you'd like to play ball with the law?"
"Think it might-a been that fighter that you saw runnin' that night?"
"Don't forget that you are white"

7. Arthur Dexter Bradley said, "I'm really not sure"
    Cops said, "A poor boy like you could use a break
    We got you for the motel job and we're talkin' to your friend Bello
    Now you don't wanta have to go back to jail, be a nice fellow
    You'll be doin' society a favor
    That sonofabitch is brave and gettin' braver
    We want to put his ass in stir
    We want to pin this triple murder on him
    He ain't no Gentleman Jim"

8. Rubin could take a man out with just one punch
    But he never did like to talk about it all that much
    It's my work, he'd say, and I do it for pay
    And when it's over I'd just as soon go on my way
    Up to some paradise
    Where the trout streams flow and the air is nice
    And ride a horse along a trail
    But then they took him to the jailhouse
    Where they try to turn a man into a mouse

9. All of Rubin's cards were marked in advance
    The trial was a pig-circus, he never had a chance
    The judge made Rubin's witnesses drunkards from the slums
    To the white folks who watched he was a revolutionary bum
    And to the black folks he was just a crazy nigger
    No one doubted that he pulled the trigger
    And though they could not produce the gun
    The D.A. said he was the one who did the deed
    And the all-white jury agreed

10. Rubin Carter was falsely tried
    The crime was murder "one," guess who testified?
    Bello and Bradley and they both baldly lied
    And the newspapers, they all went along for the ride
    How can the life of such a man
    Be in the palm of some fool's hand?
    To see him obviously framed
    Couldn't help but make me feel ashamed to live in a land
    Where justice is a game

11. Now all the criminals in their coats and their ties
    Are free to drink martinis and watch the sun rise
    While Rubin sits like Buddha in a ten-foot cell
    An innocent man in a living hell
    That's the story of the Hurricane
    But it won't be over till they clear his name
    And give him back the time he's done
    Put in a prison cell, but one time he could-a been
    The champion of the world

It Ain't Me Babe

Words and Music by Bob Dylan

G tuning:
(5th-1st) G-D-G-B-D

Key of G

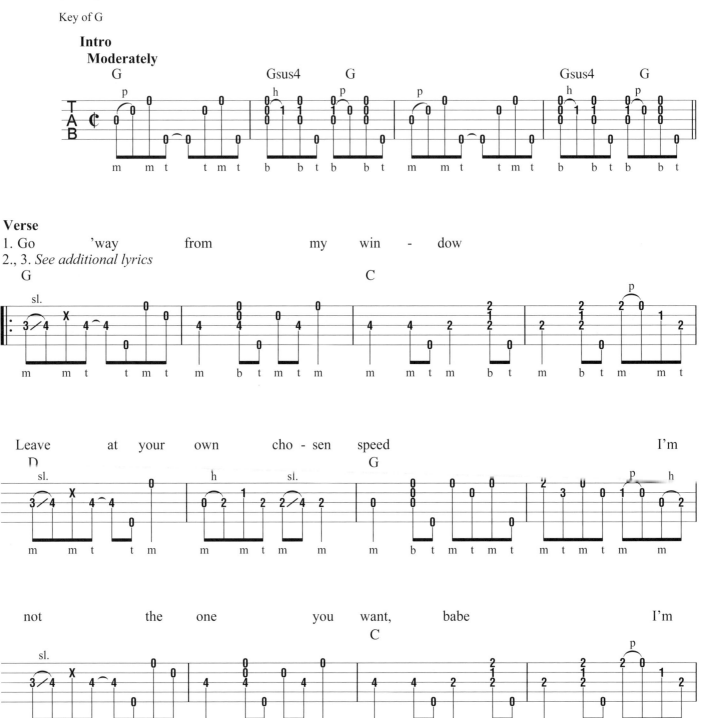

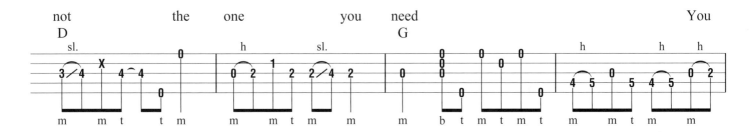

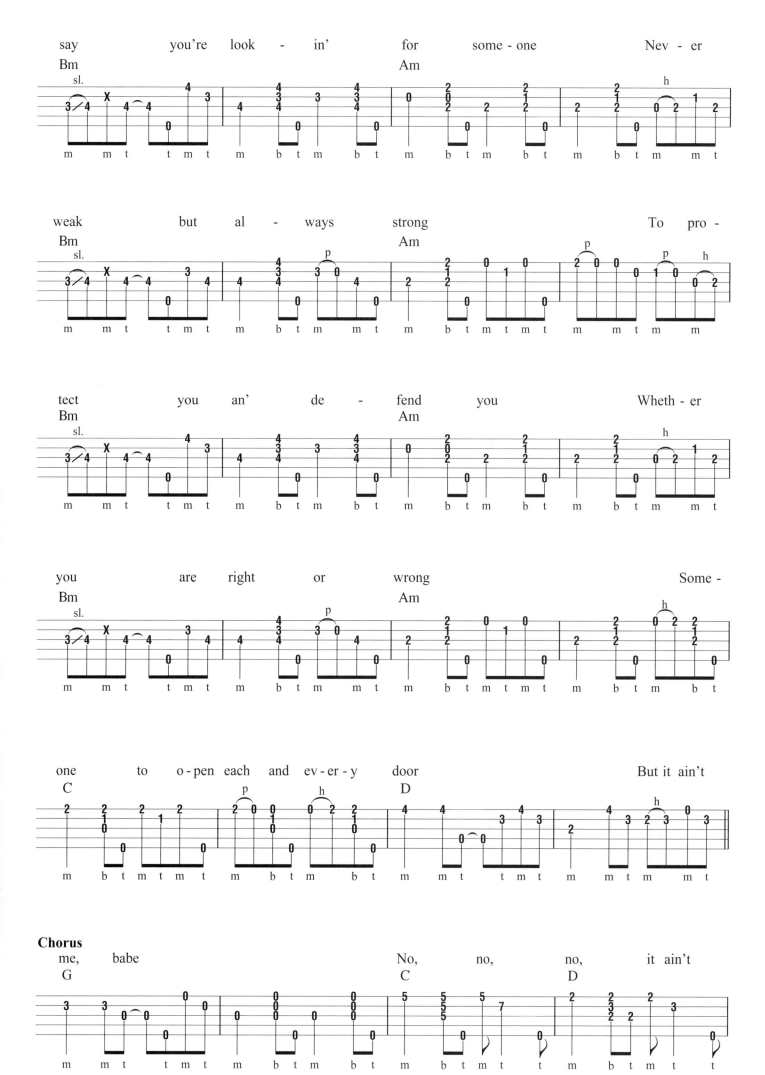

Chorus

me,   babe   It   ain't   me   you're   look - in' for,

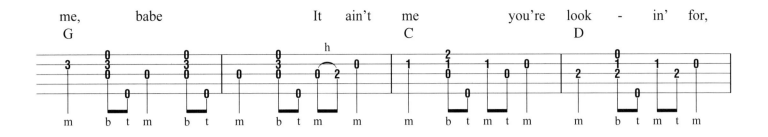

babe

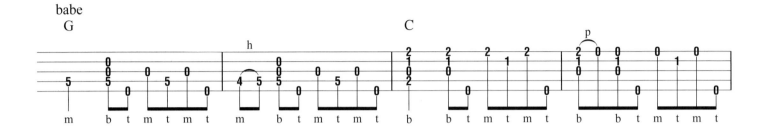

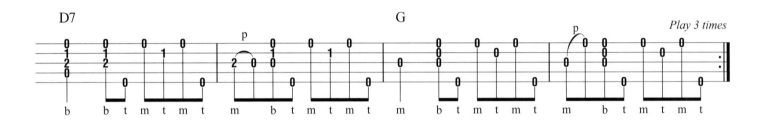

Play 3 times

Interlude

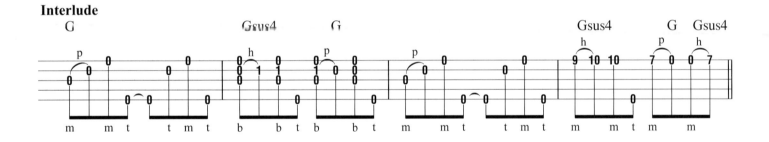

Banjo Break

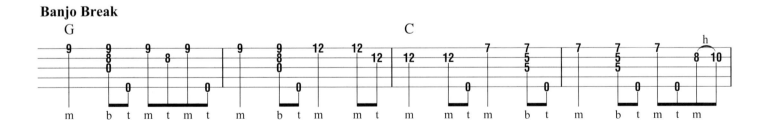

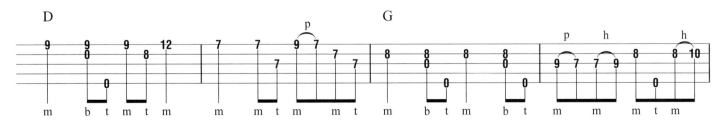

C

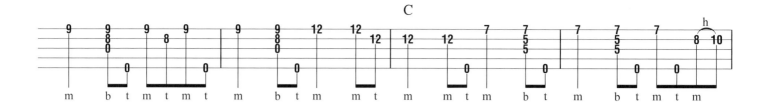

D   G

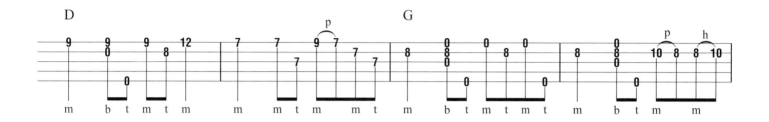

Bm   Am

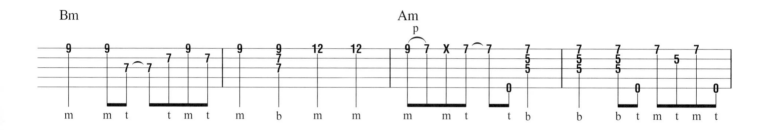

Bm   Am

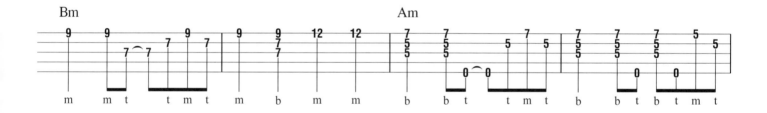

Bm   Am

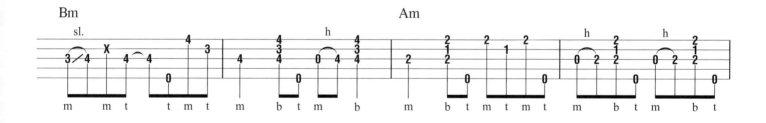

Bm   Am

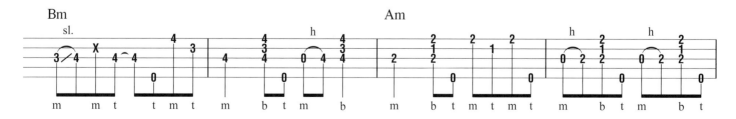

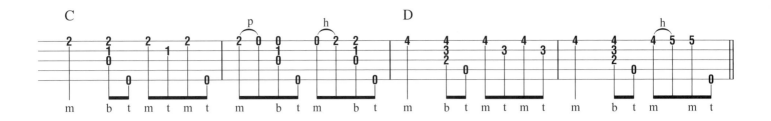

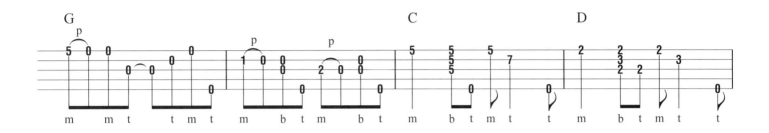

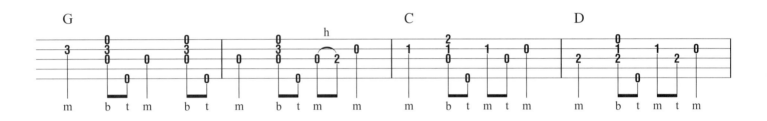

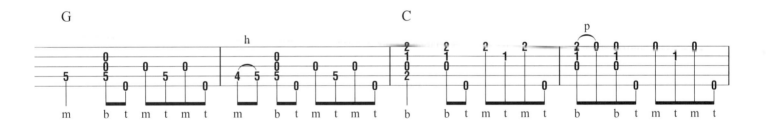

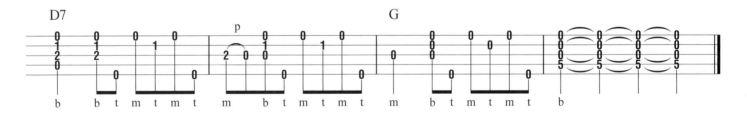

Additional Lyrics

2. Go lightly from the ledge, babe
   Go lightly on the ground
   I'm not the one you want, babe
   I will only let you down
   You say you're lookin' for someone
   Who will promise never to part
   Someone to close his eyes for you
   Someone to close his heart
   Someone who will die for you an' more

3. Go melt back into the night, babe
   Everything inside is made of stone
   There's nothing in here moving
   An' anyway I'm not alone
   You say you're lookin' for someone
   Who'll pick you up each time you fall
   To gather flowers constantly
   An' to come each time you call
   A lover for your life an' nothing more

Knockin' on Heaven's Door

Words and Music by Bob Dylan

G tuning:
(5th-1st) G-D-G-B-D

Key of G

Intro
Slow

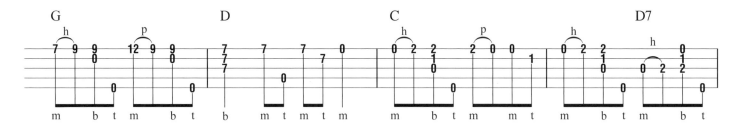

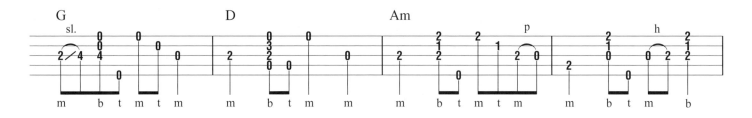

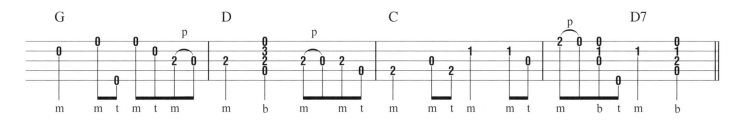

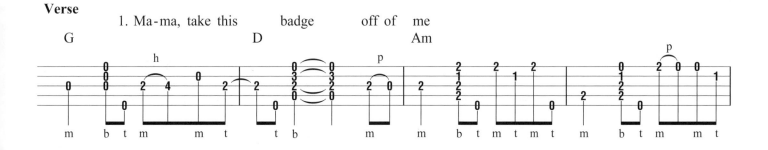

Verse

1. Ma-ma, take this badge off of me

I can't use it an-y-more

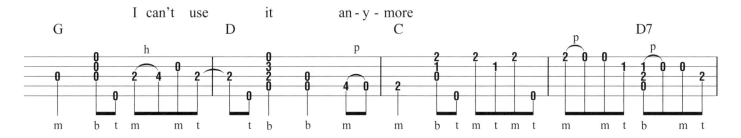

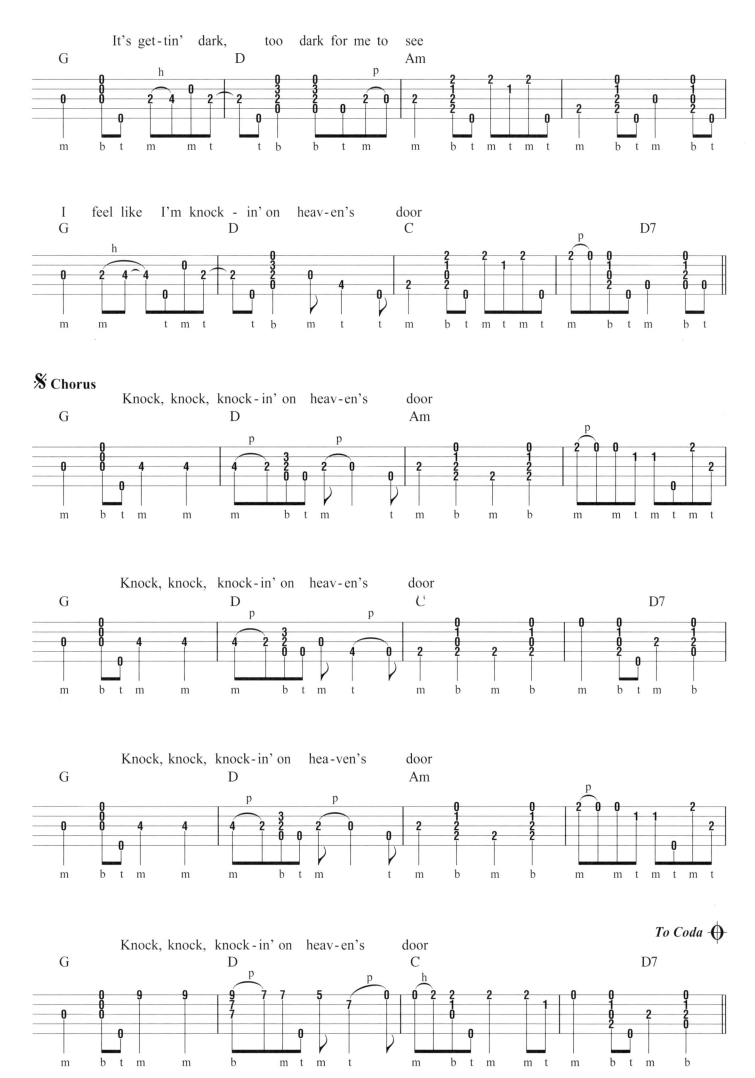

Verse

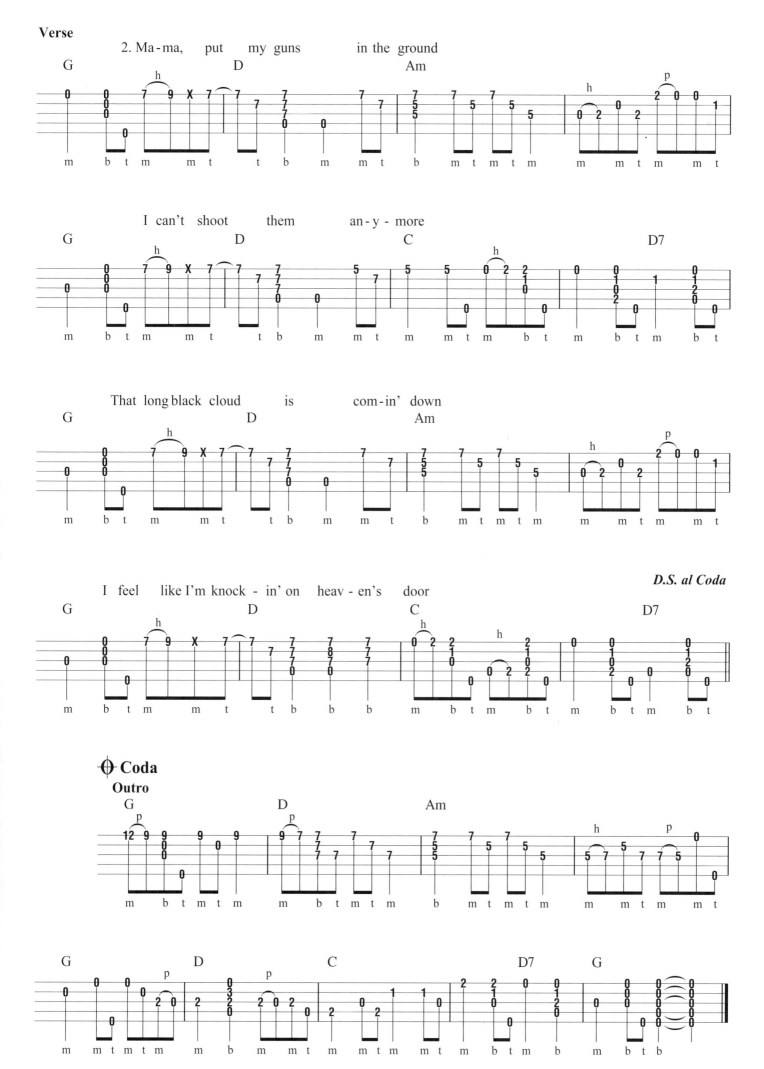

D.S. al Coda

Coda

Outro

Lay, Lady, Lay

Words and Music by Bob Dylan

G tuning:
(5th-1st) G-D-G-B-D

Key of G

Intro
Moderately slow

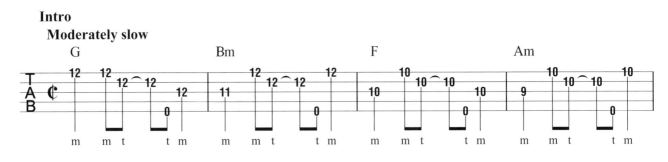

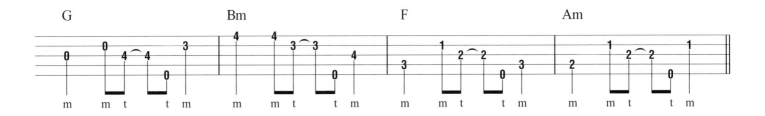

𝄋 Verse

1. Lay, la - dy, lay,   lay a - cross   my big   brass
2., 3. *See additional lyrics*

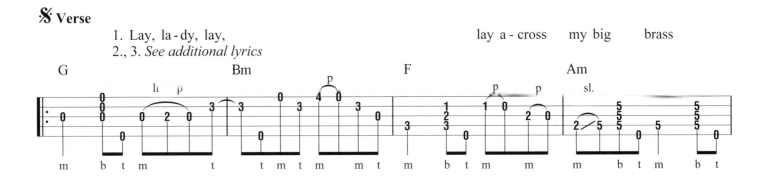

bed

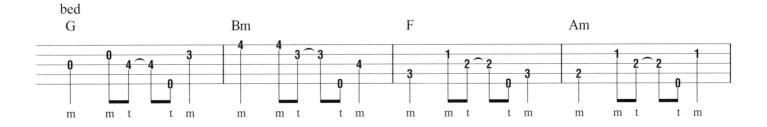

Lay, la - dy, lay,   lay a - cross   my big   brass

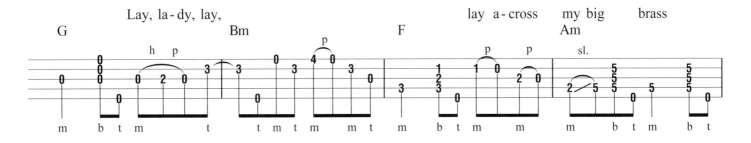

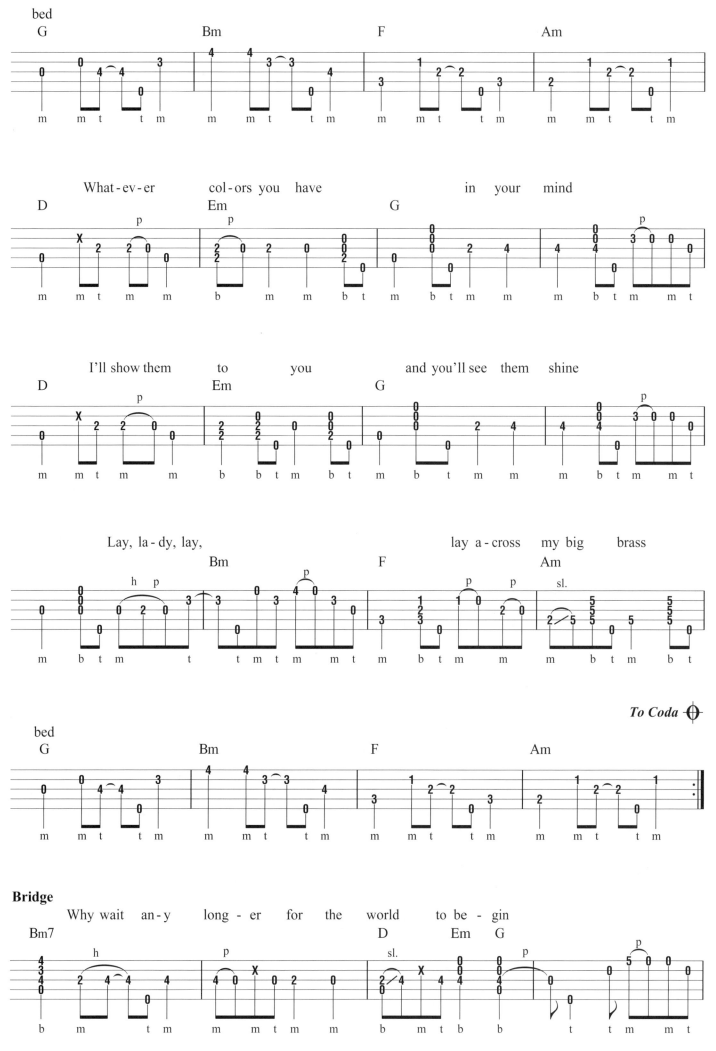

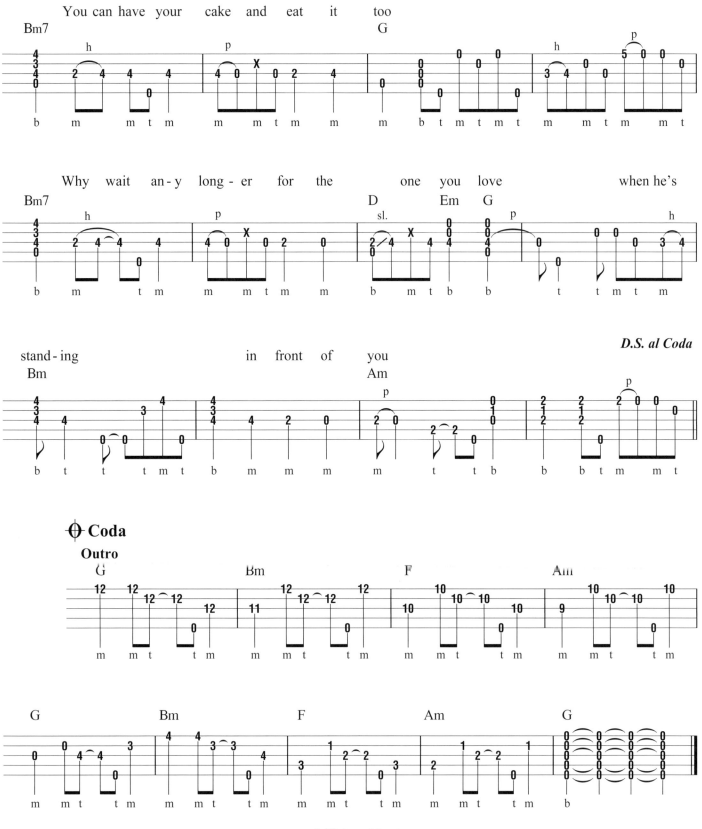

Additional Lyrics

2. Stay, lady, stay, stay with your man awhile
   Until the break of day, let me see you make him smile
   His clothes are dirty but his hands are clean
   And you're the best thing that he's ever seen
   Stay, lady, stay, stay with your man awhile

3. Lay, lady, lay, lay across my big brass bed
   Stay, lady, stay, stay while the night is still ahead
   I long to see you in the morning light
   I long to reach for you in the night
   Stay, lady, stay, stay while the night is still ahead

Mr. Tambourine Man

Words and Music by Bob Dylan

Double C tuning:
(5th-1st) G-C-G-C-D

Key of C

Chorus
Moderately

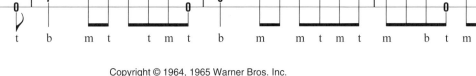

Hey! Mis-ter Tam-bou-rine Man, play a song for me I'm not
F G C F

sleep-y and there is no place I'm go-ing to
C F G

Hey! Mis-ter Tam-bou-rine Man, play a song for me In the
F G C F

jing-le jang-le morn-ing I'll come fol - low-in' you 1. Though I
C F G C

Verse
know that eve-nin's em-pire has re-turned in-to sand
2., 3. 4. *See additional lyrics*
F G C F

Copyright © 1964, 1965 Warner Bros. Inc.
Copyright Renewed 1992, 1996 Special Rider Music
International Copyright Secured   All Rights Reserved

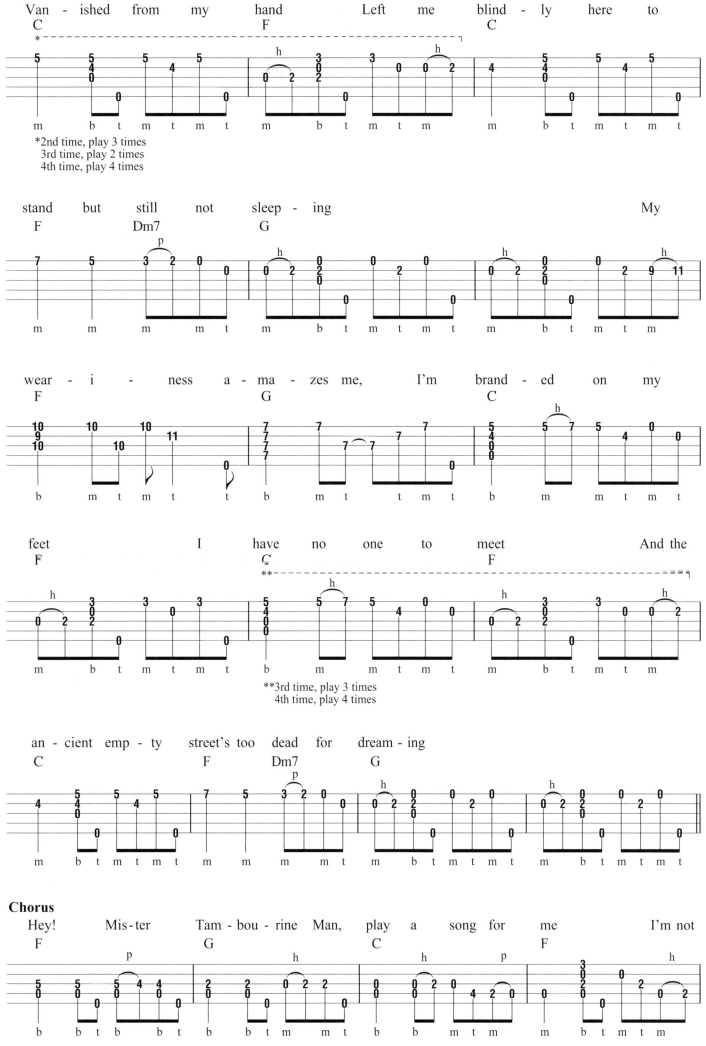

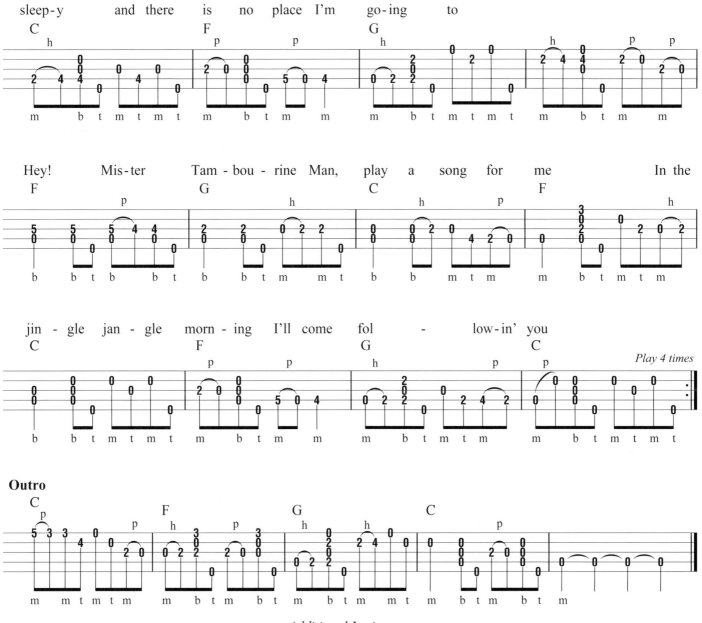

Additional Lyrics

2. Take me on a trip upon your magic swirlin' ship
My senses have been stripped, my hands can't feel to grip
My toes too numb to step
Wait only for my boot heels to be wanderin'
I'm ready to go anywhere, I'm ready for to fade
Into my own parade, cast your dancing spell my way
I promise to go under it

3. Though you might hear laughin', spinnin', swingin' madly across the sun
It's not aimed at anyone, it's just escapin' on the run
And but for the sky there are no fences facin'
And if you hear vague traces of skippin' reels of rhyme
To your tambourine in time, it's just a ragged clown behind
I wouldn't pay it any mind
It's just a shadow you're seein' that he's chasing

4. Then take me disappearin' through the smoke rings of my mind
Down the foggy ruins of time, far past the frozen leaves
The haunted, frightened trees, out to the windy beach
Far from the twisted reach of crazy sorrow
Yes, to dance beneath the diamond sky with one hand waving free
Silhouetted by the sea, circled by the circus sands
With all memory and fate driven deep beneath the waves
Let me forget about today until tomorrow

Like a Rolling Stone

Words and Music by Bob Dylan

Double C tuning:
(5th-1st) G-C-G-C-D

Key of C

Intro

Moderately

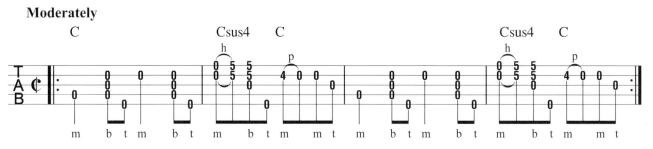

𝄋 Verse

1. Once up-on a time   you   dressed so   fine   You threw the bums a dime   in   your   prime,
3. *See additional lyrics*

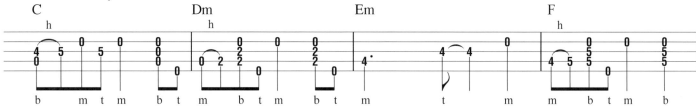

didn't   you?

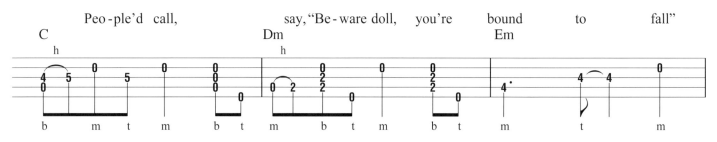

Peo-ple'd   call,   say, "Be-ware doll,   you're   bound   to   fall"

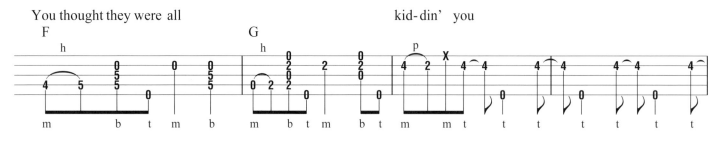

You thought they were all   kid-din' you

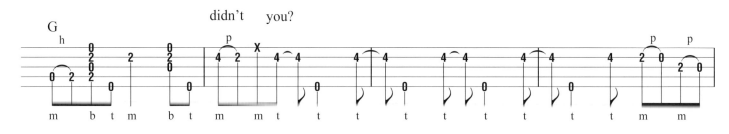

You   used   to   laugh a - bout

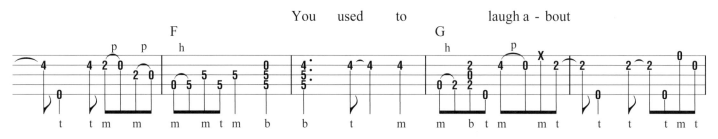

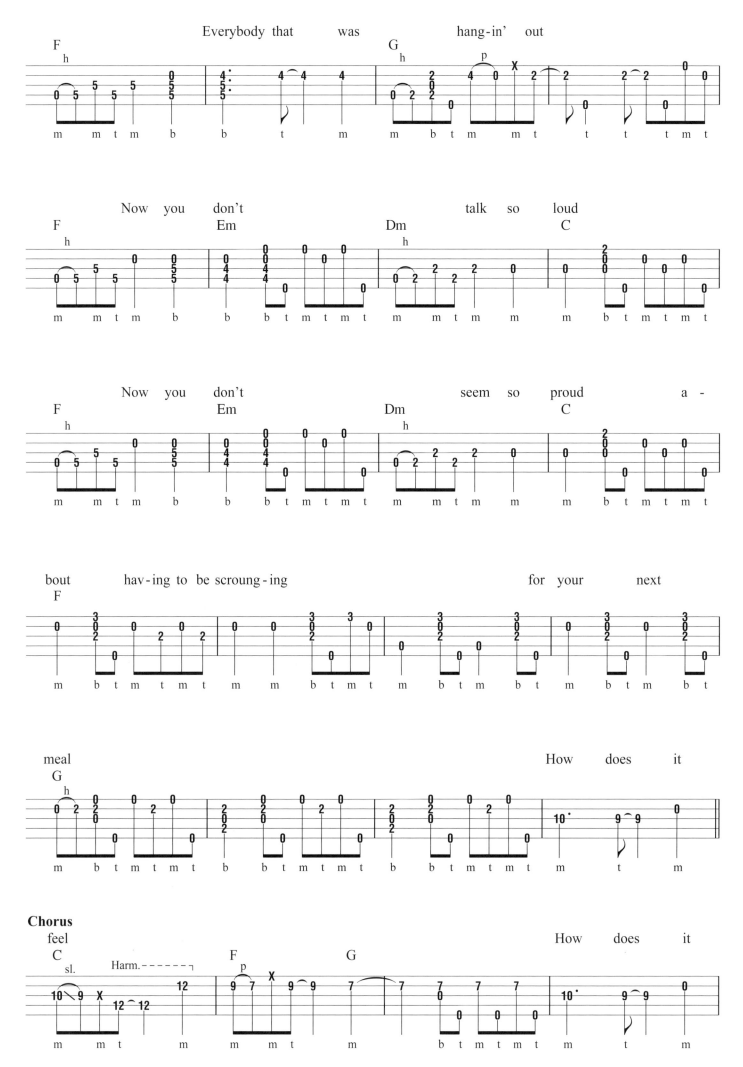

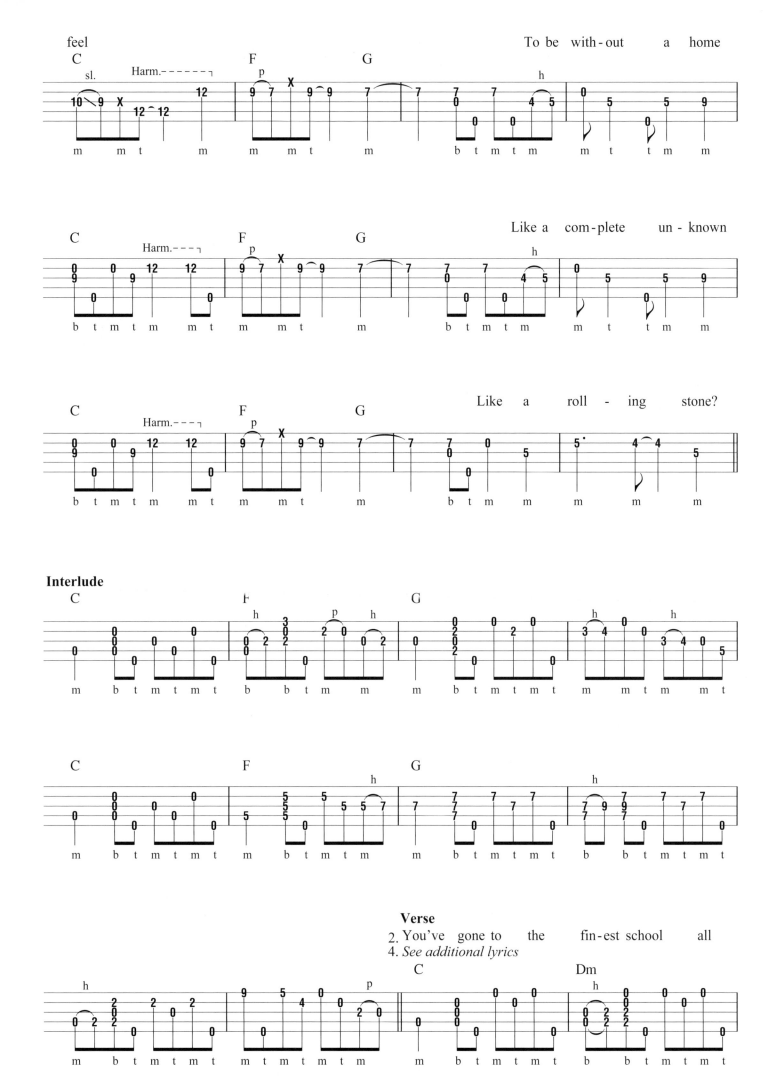

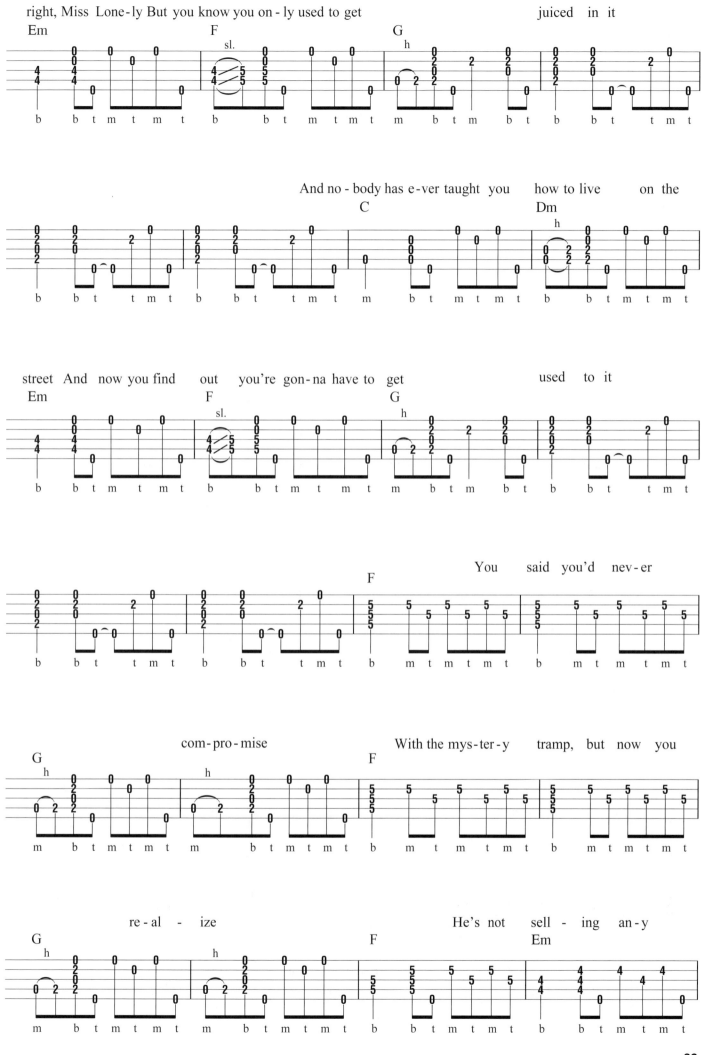

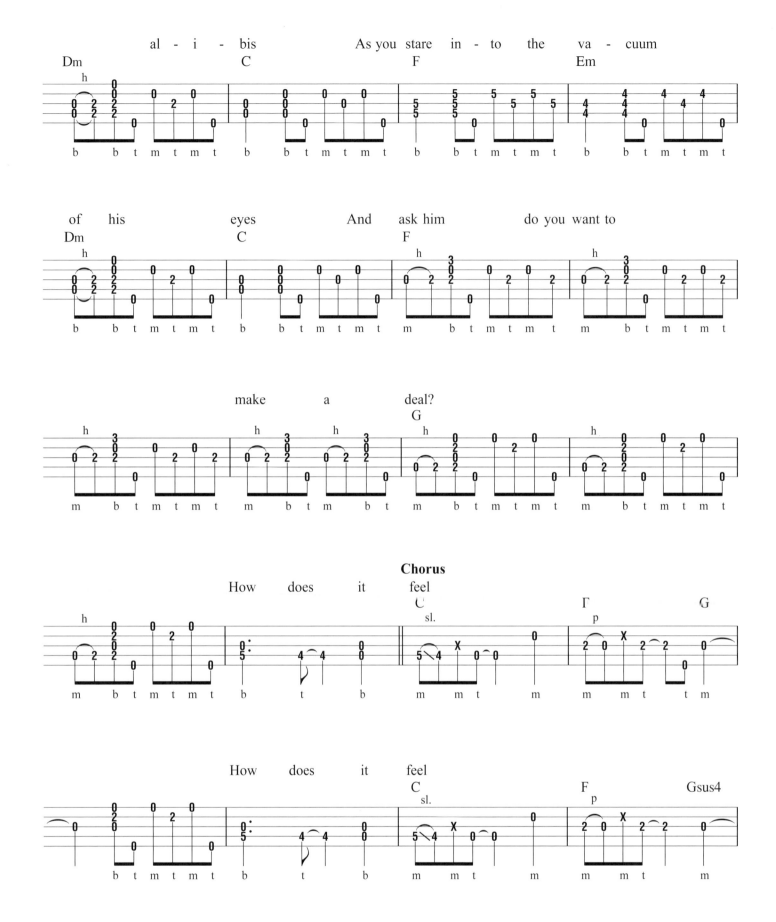

Chorus

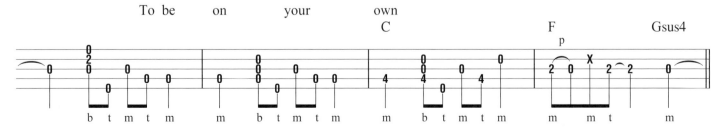

With no di - rect - ion home
Like a com - plete un - known

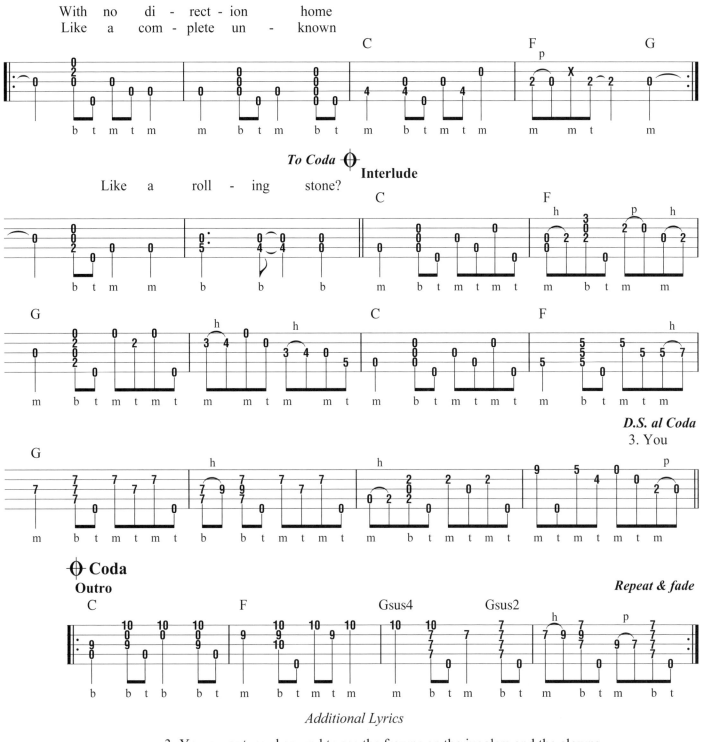

Like a roll - ing stone?

Additional Lyrics

3. You never turned around to see the frowns on the jugglers and the clowns
When they all come down and did tricks for you
You never understood that it ain't no good
You shouldn't let other people get your kicks for you
You used to ride on the chrome horse with your diplomat
Who carried on his shoulder a Siamese cat
Ain't it hard when you discover that
He really wasn't where it's at
After he took from you everthing he could steal

4. Princess on the steeple and all the pretty people
They're drinkin', thinkin' that they got it made
Exchanging all kinds of precious gifts and things
But you'd better lift your diamond ring, you'd better pawn it babe
You used to be so amused
At Napoleon in rags and the language that he used
Go to him now, he calls you, you can't refuse
When you got nothing, you got nothing to lose
You're invisible now, you got no secrets to conceal

Positively 4th Street

Words and Music by Bob Dylan

D tuning:
(5th-1st) A-D-F#-A-D

Key of D

Intro
Moderately

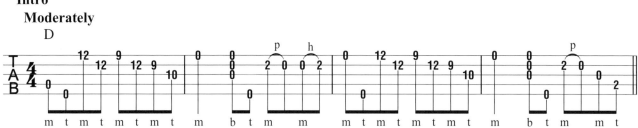

Verse

1. You got a lot-ta nerve To say you are my friend
5., 9. *See additional lyrics*

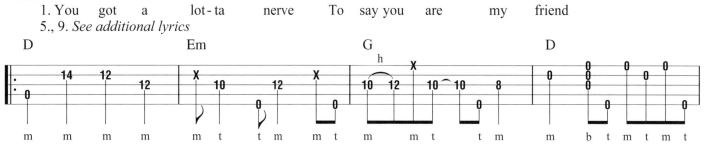

When I was down   You just   stood there   grin-ning

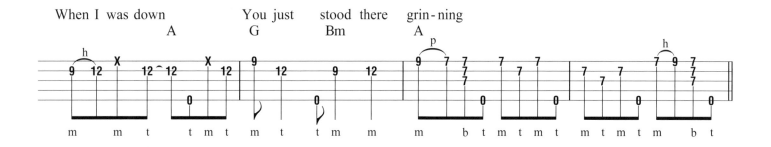

Verse

2. You got a lot-ta nerve To say you got a help-ing hand to lend
6., 10. *See additional lyrics*

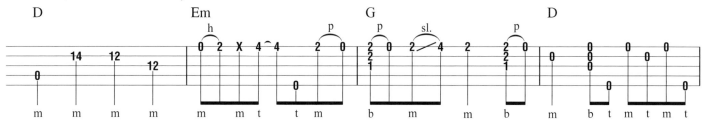

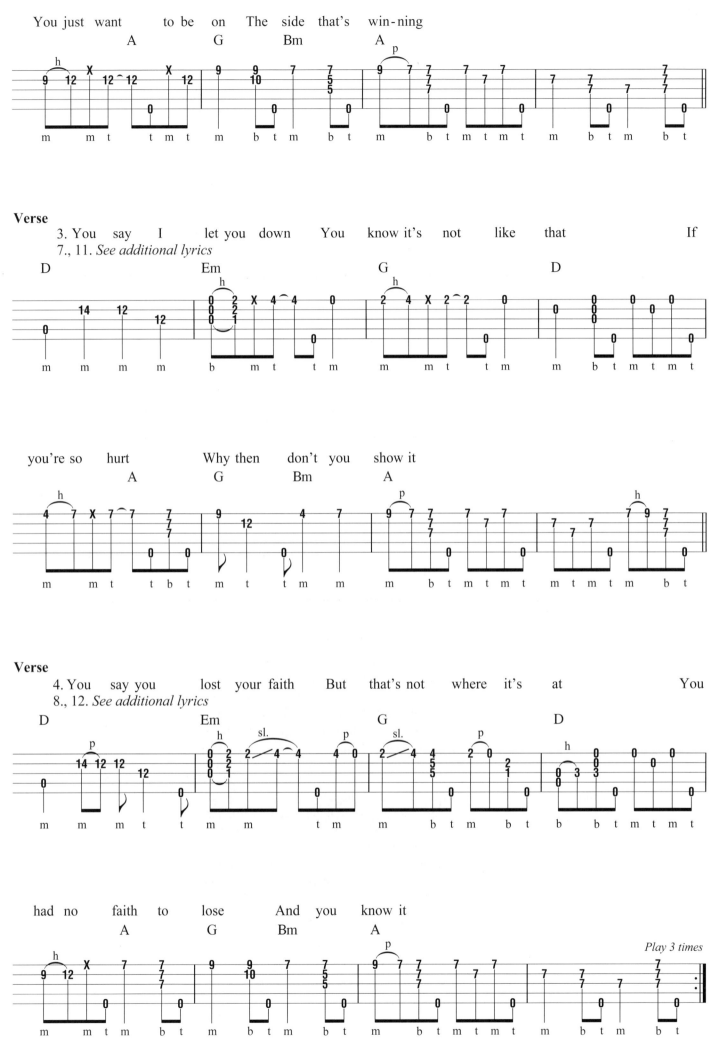

Outro

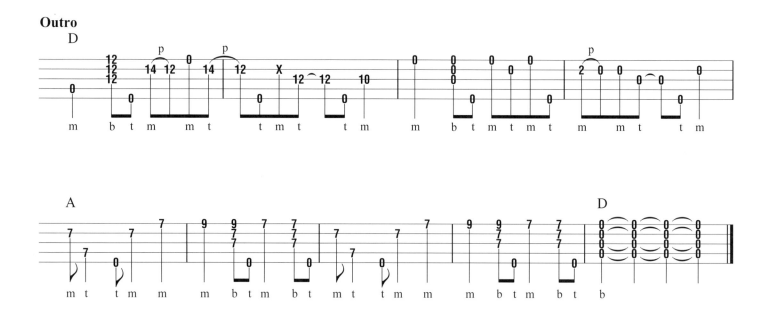

Additional Lyrics

5. I know the reason
That you talk behind my back
I used to be among the crowd
You're in with

6. Do you take me for such a fool
To think I'd make contact
With the one who tries to hide
What he don't know to begin with

7. You see me on the street
You always act surprised
You say, "How are you?" "Good luck"
But you don't mean it

8. When you know as well as me
You'd rather see me paralyzed
Why don't you just come out once
And scream it

9. No, I do not feel that good
When I see the heartbreaks you embrace
If I was a master thief
Perhaps I'd rob them

10. And now I know you're dissatisfied
With your position and your place
Don't you understand
It's not my problem

11. I wish that for just one time
You could stand inside my shoes
And just for that one moment
I could be you

12. Yes, I wish that for just one time
You could stand inside my shoes
You'd know what a drag it is
To see you

Tangled Up in Blue

Words and Music by Bob Dylan

D tuning:
(5th-1st) A-D-F#-A-D

Key of D

Intro

Moderately slow

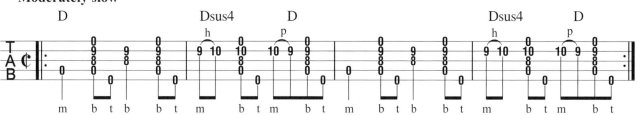

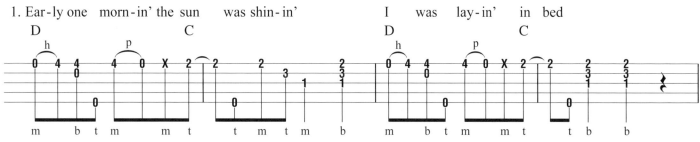

Verse

1. Ear-ly one morn-in' the sun was shin-in' I was lay-in' in bed

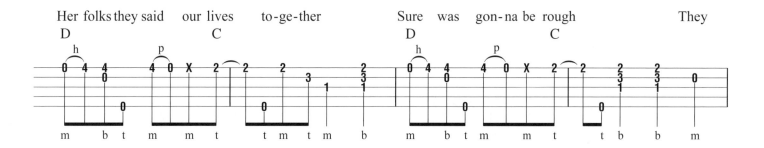

Won - d'rin' if she'd changed at all If her hair was still red

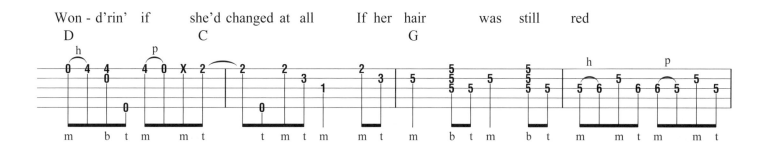

Her folks they said our lives to-ge-ther Sure was gon-na be rough They

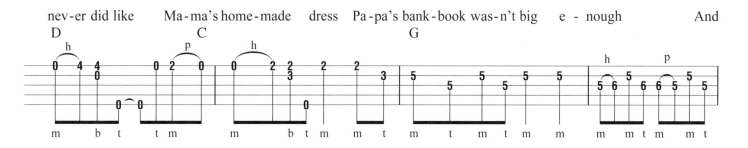

nev-er did like Ma-ma's home-made dress Pa-pa's bank-book was-n't big e - nough And

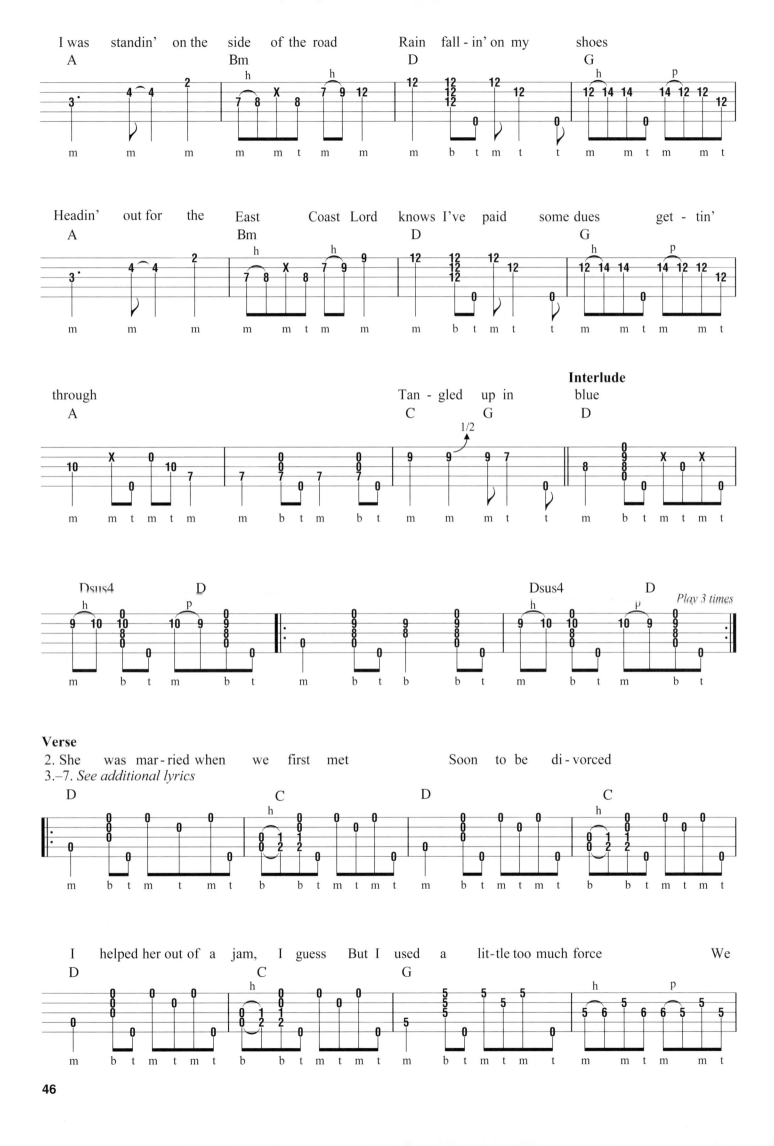

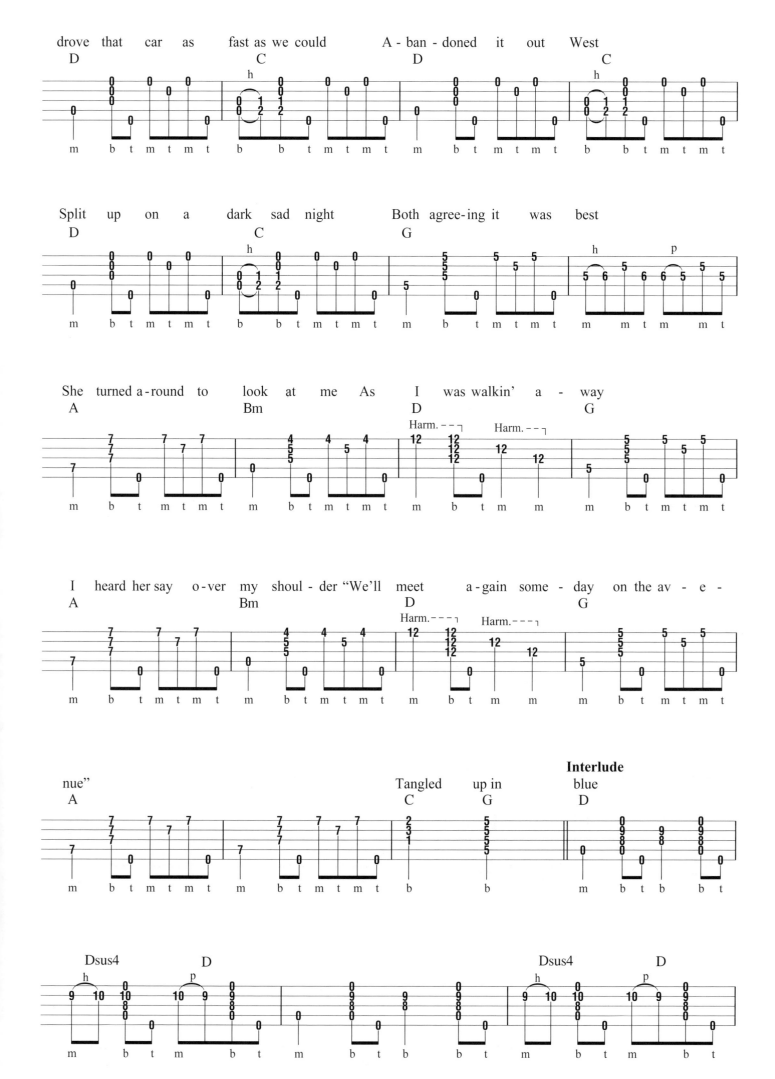

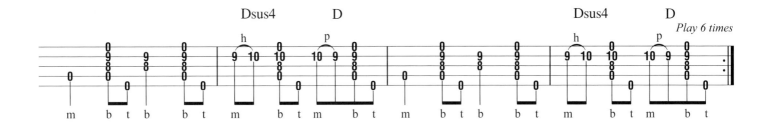

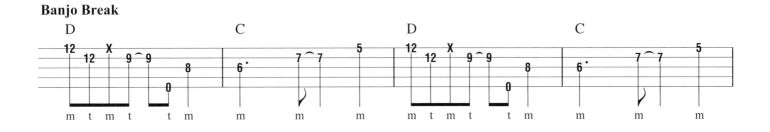

Banjo Break

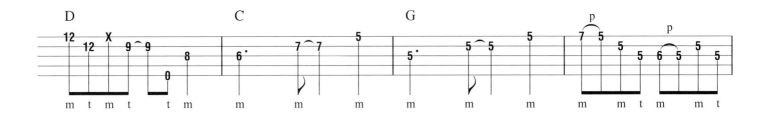

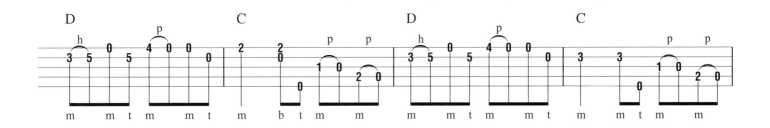

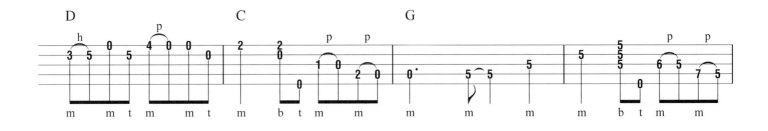

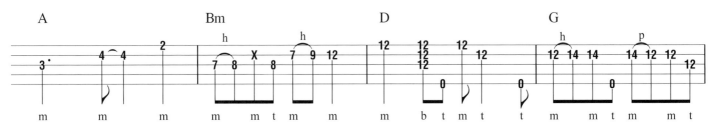

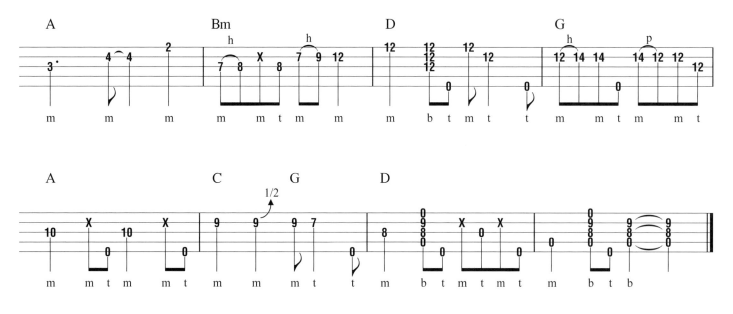

Additional Lyrics

3. I had a job in the great north woods
   Working as a cook for a spell
   But I never did like it all that much
   And one day the ax just fell
   So I drifted down to New Orleans
   Where I happened to be employed
   Workin' for a while on a fishin' boat
   Right outside of Delacroix
   But all the while I was alone
   The past was close behind
   I seen a lot of women
   But she never escaped my mind, and I just grew
   Tangled up in blue

4. She was workin' in a topless place
   And I stopped in for a beer
   I just kept lookin' at the side of her face
   In the spotlight so clear
   And later on as the crowd thinned out
   I's just about to do the same
   She was standing there in back of my chair
   Said to me, "Don't I know your name?"
   I muttered somethin' underneath my breath
   She studied the lines on my face
   I must admit I felt a little uneasy
   When she bent down to tie the laces of my shoe
   Tangled up in blue

5. She lit a burner on the stove
   And offered me a pipe
   "I thought you'd never say hello," she said
   "You look like the silent type"
   Then she opened up a book of poems
   And handed it to me
   Written by an Italian poet
   From the thirteenth century
   And every one of them words rang true
   And glowed like burnin' coal
   Pourin' off of every page
   Like it was written in my soul from me to you
   Tangled up in blue

6. I lived with them on Montague Street
   In a basement down the stairs
   There was music in the cafés at night
   And revolution in the air
   Then he started into dealing with slaves
   And something inside of him died
   She had to sell everything she owned
   And froze up inside
   And when finally the bottom fell out
   I became withdrawn
   The only thing I knew how to do
   Was to keep on keepin' on like a bird that flew
   Tangled up in blue

7. So now I'm goin' back again
   I got to get to her somehow
   All the people we used to know
   They're an illusion to me now
   Some are mathematicians
   Some are carpenters' wives
   Don't know how it all got started
   I don't know what they're doin' with their lives
   But me, I'm still on the road
   Headin' for another joint
   We always did feel the same
   We just saw it from a different point of view
   Tangled up in blue

Shelter from the Storm

Words and Music by Bob Dylan

D tuning:
(5th-1st) A-D-F#-A-D

Key of D

Intro

Moderately

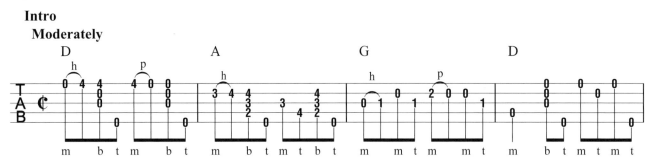

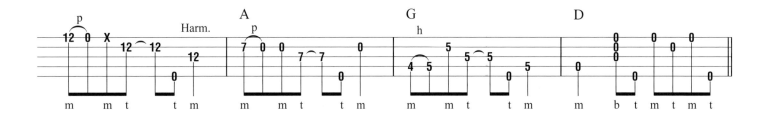

𝄋 Verse

1. 'Twas   in an-oth-er   life-time,   one   of toil   and   blood   When
3., 5., 7., 9. *See additional lyrics*

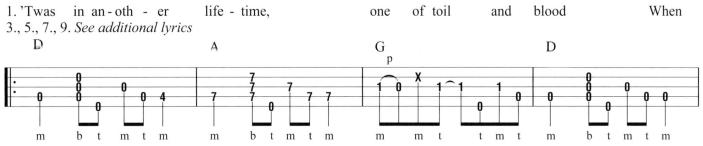

black-ness   was   a   vir-tue   and the road was full   of   mud   I

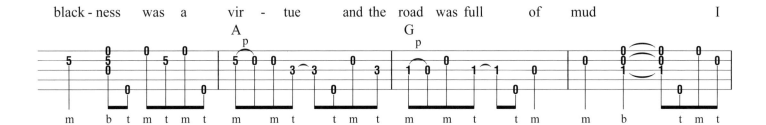

came in   from the   wil-der-ness,   a   crea-ture void of   form   "Come

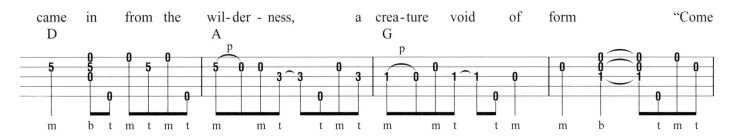

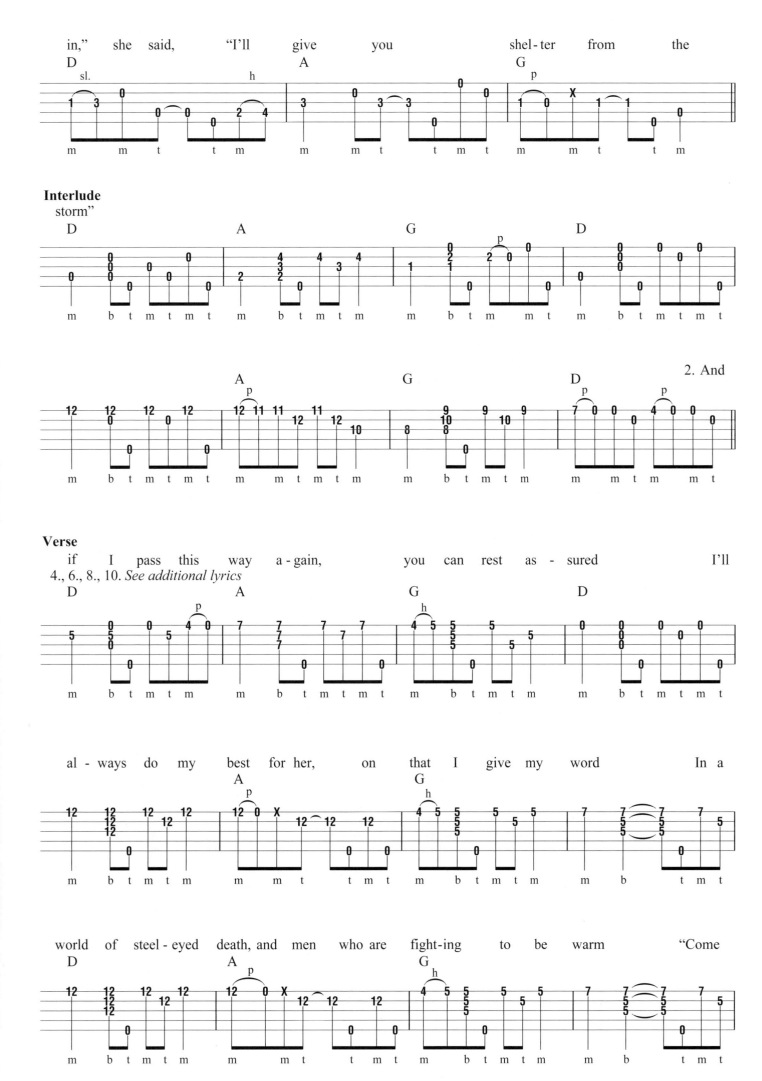

in," she said, "I'll give you shel - ter from the

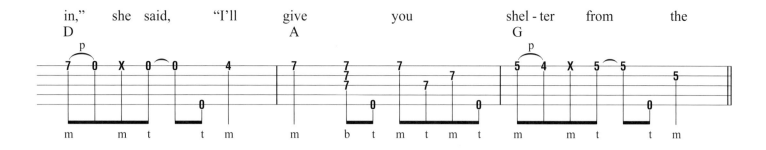

Interlude

storm"

To Coda ⊕

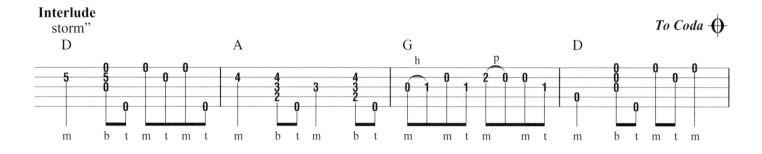

4th time, D.S. al Coda

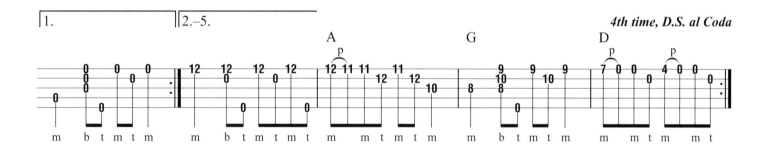

⊕ **Coda**

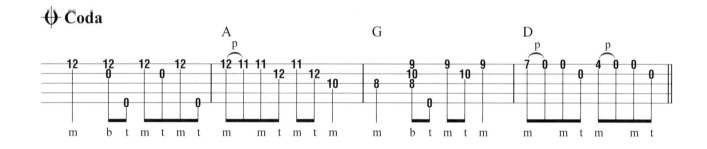

Outro

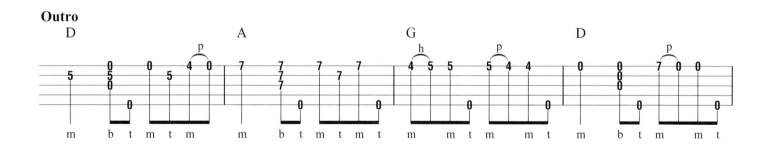

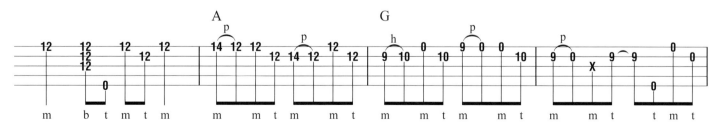

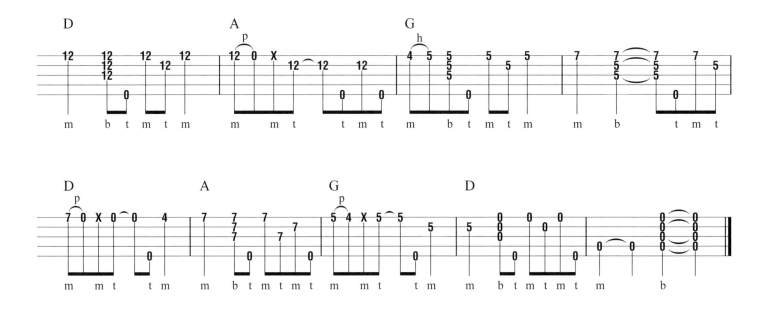

Additional Lyrics

3. Not a word was spoke between us, there was little risk involved
   Everything up to that point had been left unresolved
   Try imagining a place where it's always safe and warm
   "Come in," she said, "I'll give you shelter from the storm"

4. I was burned out from exhaustion, buried in the hail
   Poisoned in the bushes an' blown out on the trail
   Hunted like a crocodile, ravaged in the corn
   "Come in," she said, "I'll give you shelter from the storm"

5. Suddenly I turned around and she was standin' there
   With silver bracelets on her wrists and flowers in her hair
   She walked up to me so gracefully and took my crown of thorns
   "Come in," she said, "I'll give you shelter from the storm"

6. Now there's a wall between us, somethin' there's been lost
   I took too much for granted, got my signals crossed
   Just to think that it all began on a long-forgotten morn
   "Come in," she said, "I'll give you shelter from the storm"

7. Well, the deputy walks on hard nails and the preacher rides a mount
   But nothing really matters much, it's doom alone that counts
   And the one-eyed undertaker, he blows a futile horn
   "Come in," she said, "I'll give you shelter from the storm"

8. I've heard newborn babies wailin' like a mournin' dove
   And old men with broken teeth stranded without love
   Do I understand your question, man, is it hopeless and forlorn?
   "Come in," she said, "I'll give you shelter from the storm"

9. In a little hilltop village, they gambled for my clothes
   I bargained for salvation an' they gave me a lethal dose
   I offered up my innocence and got repaid with scorn
   "Come in," she said, "I'll give you shelter from the storm"

10. Well, I'm livin' in a foreign country but I'm bound to cross the line
    Beauty walks a razor's edge, someday I'll make it mine
    If I could only turn back the clock to when God and her were born
    "Come in," she said, "I'll give you shelter from the storm"

The Times They Are A-Changin'

Words and Music by Bob Dylan

Double C tuning:
(5th-1st) G-C-G-C-D

Key of C

Verse
Slow in 1

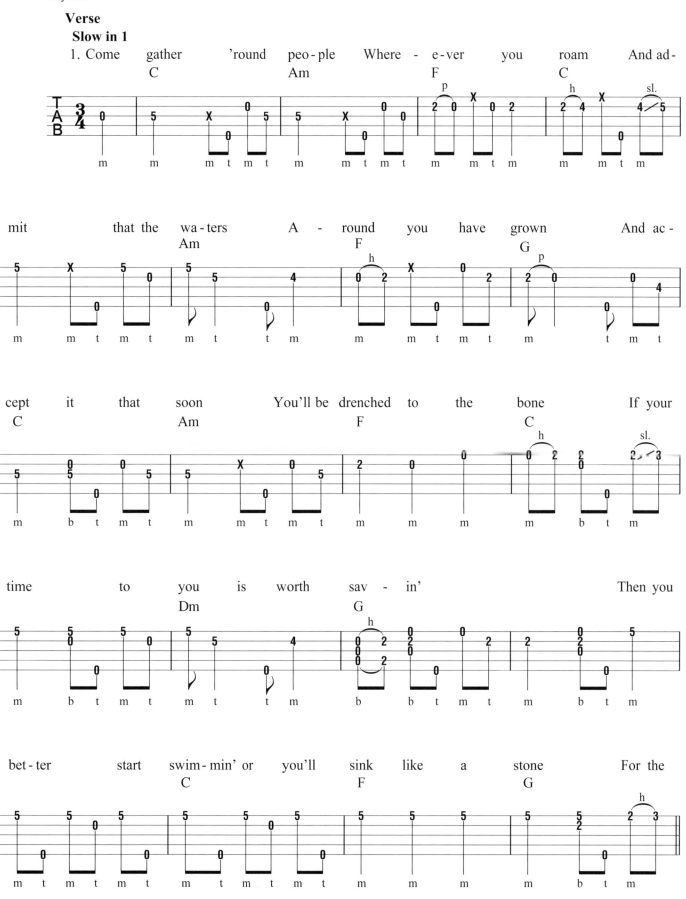

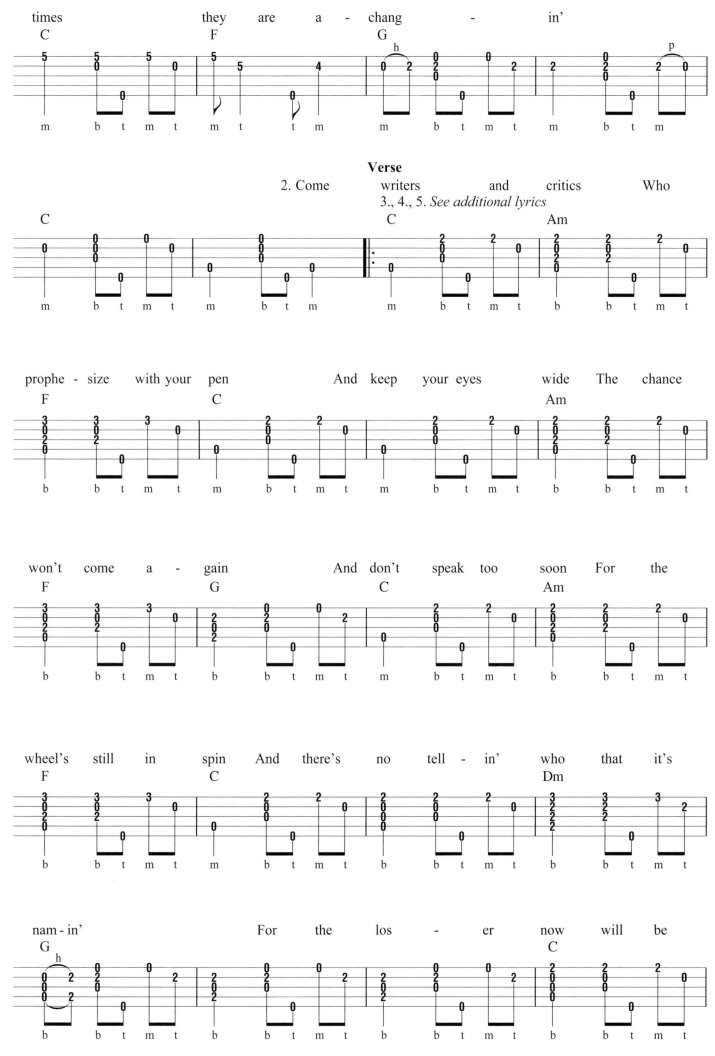

lat - er to win For the times they are a -

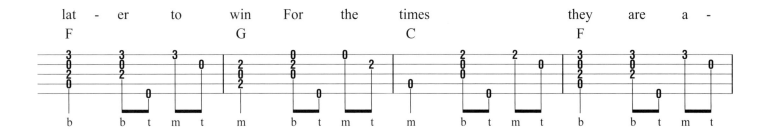

chang - in' 3. Come

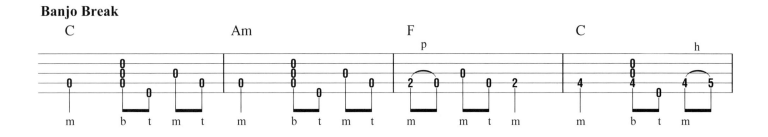

Banjo Break

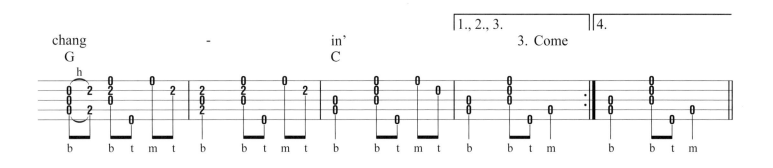

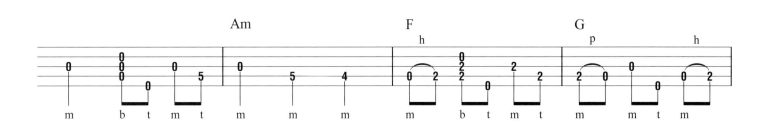

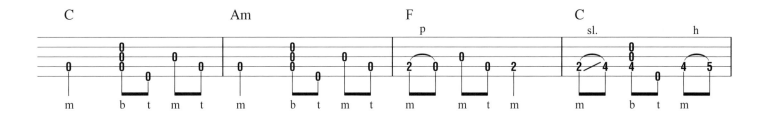

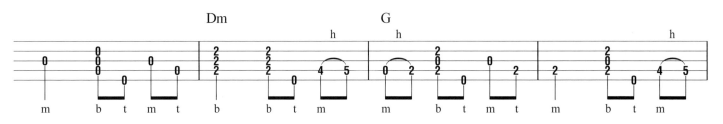

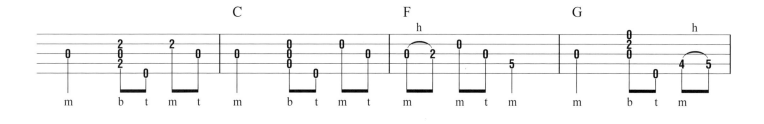

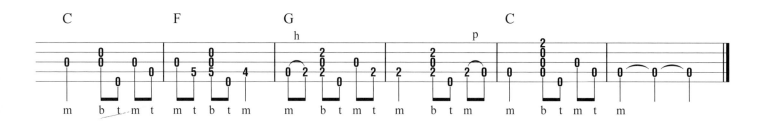

Additional Lyrics

3. Come senators, congressmen
   Please heed the call
   Don't stand in the doorway
   Don't block up the hall
   For he that gets hurt
   Will be he who has stalled
   There's a battle outside and it is ragin'
   It'll soon shake your windows and rattle your walls
   For the times they are a-changin'

4. Come mothers and fathers
   Throughout the land
   And don't criticize
   What you can't understand
   Your sons and your daughters
   Are beyond your command
   Your old road is rapidly agin'
   Please get out of the new one if you can't lend your hand
   For the times they are a-changin'

5. The line it is drawn
   The curse it is cast
   The slow one now
   Will later be fast
   As the present now
   Will later be past
   The order is rapidly fadin'
   And the first one now will later be last
   For the times they are a-changin'

You Ain't Goin' Nowhere

Words and Music by Bob Dylan

G tuning:
(5th-1st) G-D-G-B-D

Key of G

Intro
Moderately slow

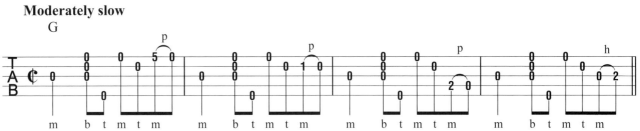

Verse

1. Clouds so swift   Rain won't lift   Gate won't close   Rail - ings froze
3. Buy   me a flute And a   gun   that shoots   Tail - gates   and   sub - sti - tutes

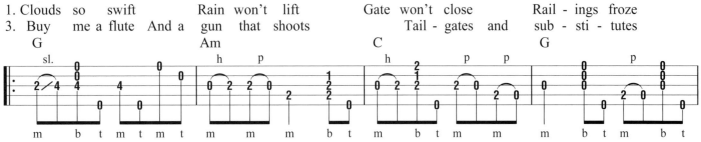

Get   your mind   off   win - ter - time)
Strap   your - self To the tree   with roots)   You   ain't go - in' no - where

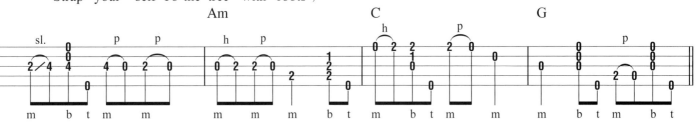

Chorus

Whoo - ee!   Ride   me high   To - mor - row's the day My   bride's gon - na come

Oh, oh, are we gon-na fly Down in the ea - sy chair!

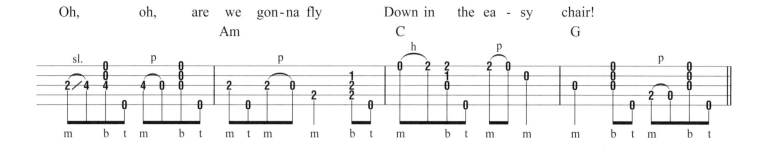

Interlude

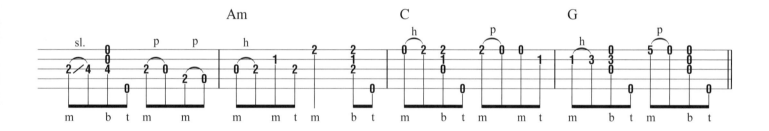

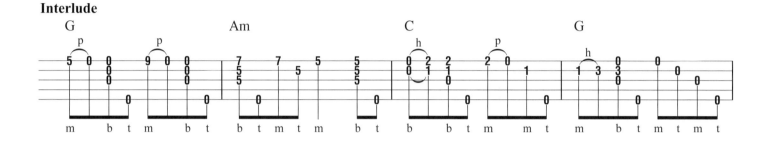

Verse

2. I don't care How man-y let-ters they sent Morn - ing came and morn - ing went
4. Gen - ghis Khan He could not keep All his kings Sup - plied with sleep We'll

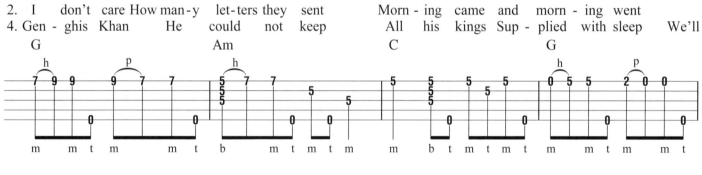

Pick up your mon-ey And pack up your tent You ain't go-in' no - where
climb that hill no mat-ter how steep When we get up to it

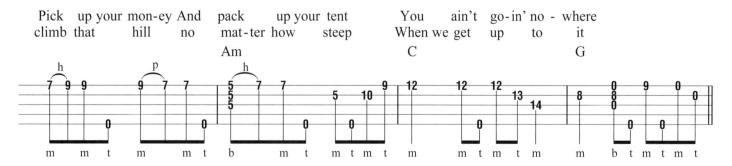

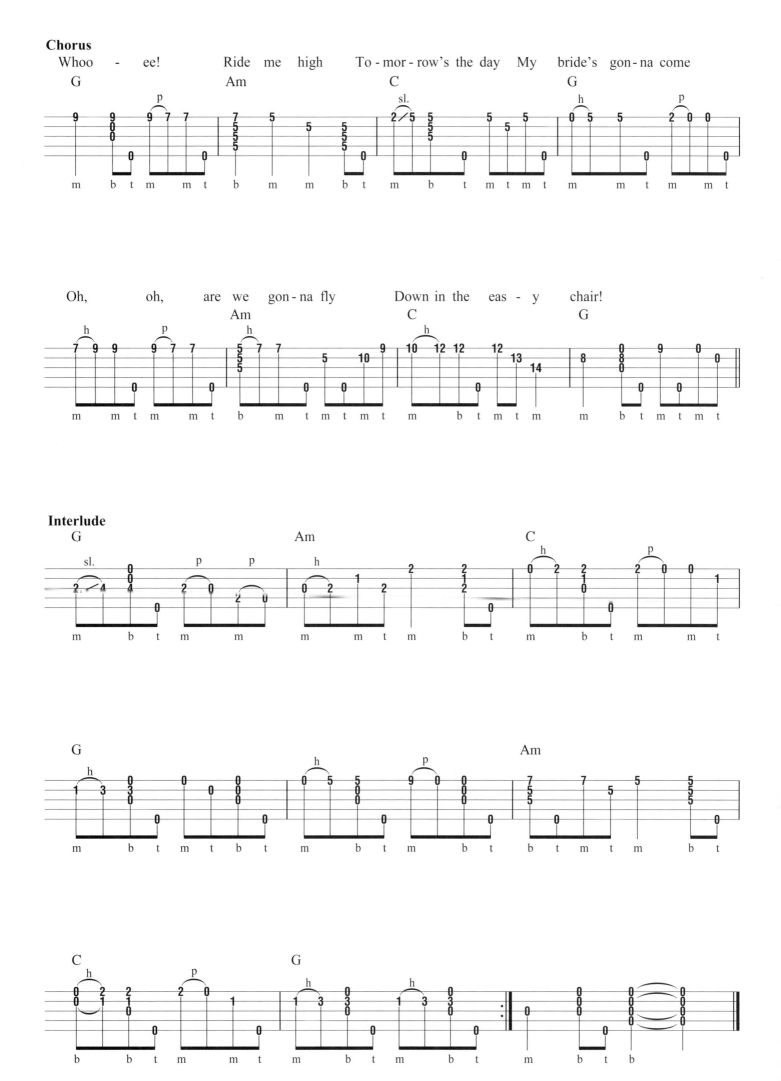

Hal•Leonard BANJO PLAY-ALONG

The Banjo Play-Along Series will help you play your favorite songs quickly and easily with incredible backing tracks to help you sound like a bona fide pro! Just follow the banjo tab, listen to the demo audio track provided to hear how the banjo should sound, and then play along with the separate backing tracks.

Each Banjo Play-Along pack features eight cream of the crop songs.

1. BLUEGRASS

Ashland Breakdown • Deputy Dalton • Dixie Breakdown • Hickory Hollow • I Wish You Knew • I Wonder Where You Are Tonight • Love and Wealth • Salt Creek.
00102585 Book/CD Pack $16.99

2. COUNTRY

East Bound and Down • Flowers on the Wall • Gentle on My Mind • Highway 40 Blues • If You've Got the Money (I've Got the Time) • Just Because • Take It Easy • You Are My Sunshine.
00105278 Book/CD Pack $14.99

3. FOLK/ROCK HITS

Ain't It Enough • The Cave • Forget the Flowers • Ho Hey • Little Lion Man • Live and Die • Switzerland • Wagon Wheel.
00119867 Book/CD Pack $14.99

4. OLD-TIME CHRISTMAS

Away in a Manger • Hark! the Herald Angels Sing • Jingle Bells • Joy to the World • O Holy Night • O Little Town of Bethlehem • Silent Night • We Wish You a Merry Christmas.
00119889 Book/CD Pack $14.99

5. PETE SEEGER
Blue Skies • Get up and Go • If I Had a Hammer (The Hammer Song) • Kisses Sweeter Than Wine • Mbube (Wimoweh) • Sailing Down My Golden River • Turn! Turn! Turn! (To Everything There Is a Season) • We Shall Overcome.
00129699 Book/CD Pack $17.99

6. SONGS FOR BEGINNERS

Bill Cheatham • Black Mountain Rag • Cripple Creek • Grandfather's Clock • John Hardy • Nine Pound Hammer • Old Joe Clark • Will the Circle Be Unbroken.
00139751 Book/CD Pack $14.99

7. BLUEGRASS GOSPEL

Cryin' Holy unto the Lord • How Great Thou Art • I Saw the Light • I'll Fly Away • I'll Have a New Life • Man in the Middle • Turn Your Radio On • Wicked Path of Sin.
00147594 Book/Online Audio $14.99

8. CELTIC BLUEGRASS

Billy in the Low Ground • Cluck Old Hen • Devil's Dream • Fisher's Hornpipe • Little Maggie • Over the Waterfall • The Red Haired Boy • Soldier's Joy.
00160077 Book/Online Audio $14.99

9. BLUEGRASS FESTIVAL FAVORITES

Banks of the Ohio • Cotton Eyed Joe • Cumberland Gap • Eighth of January • Liberty • Man of Constant Sorrow • Roll in My Sweet Baby's Arms • Wildwood Flower.
00263129 Book/Online Audio $14.99

www.halleonard.com

Prices, contents, and availability subject to change without notice.

GREAT BANJO PUBLICATIONS

FROM HAL LEONARD

Hal Leonard Banjo Method
by Mac Robertson, Robbie Clement, Will Schmid
This innovative method teaches 5-string banjo bluegrass style using a carefully paced approach that keeps beginners playing great songs *while learning*. Book 1 covers easy chord strums, tablature, right-hand rolls, hammer-ons, slides and pull-offs, and more. Book 2 includes solos and licks, fiddle tunes, back-up, capo use, and more.

00699500 Book 1 Book Only $9.99
00695101 Book 1 Book/Online Audio $17.99
00699502 Book 2 Book Only $9.99

Banjo Chord Finder
00695741 9 x 12..$8.99
00695742 6 x 9..$7.99

Banjo Scale Finder
00695783 6 x 9..$6.99

Banjo Aerobics
A 50-Week Workout Program for Developing, Improving and Maintaining Banjo Technique
by Michael Bremer
Take your banjo playing to the next level with this fantastic daily resource, providing a year's worth of practice material with a two-week vacation. The accompanying audio includes demo tracks for all the examples in the book to reinforce how the banjo should sound.
00113734 Book/Online Audio $22.99

Earl Scruggs and the 5-String Banjo
Earl Scruggs' legendary method has helped thousands of banjo players get their start. It features everything you need to know to start playing, even how to build your own banjo! Topics covered include: Scruggs tuners • how to read music • chords • how to read tablature • anatomy of Scruggs-style picking • exercises in picking • 44 songs • biographical notes • and more! The online audio features Earl Scruggs playing and explaining over 60 examples!
00695764 Book Only $29.99
00695765 Book/Online Audio $39.99

First 50 Songs You Should Play on Banjo
arr. Michael J. Miles & Greg Cahill
Easy-to-read banjo tab, chord symbols and lyrics for the most popular songs banjo players like to play. Explore clawhammer and three-finger-style banjo in a variety of tunings and capoings with this one-of-a-kind collection. Songs include: Angel from Montgomery • Carolina in My Mind • Cripple Creek • Danny Boy • The House of the Rising Sun • Mr. Tambourine Man • Take Me Home, Country Roads • This Land Is Your Land • Wildwood Flower • and many more.
00153311 ....$15.99

Fretboard Roadmaps
by Fred Sokolow
This handy book/with online audio will get you playing all over the banjo fretboard in any key! You'll learn to: increase your chord, scale and lick vocabulary • play chord-based licks, moveable major and blues scales, melodic scales and first-position major scales • and much more! The audio includes 51 demonstrations of the exercises.

00695358 Book/Online Audio $17.99

The Great American Banjo Songbook
70 Songs
arr. Alan Munde & Beth Mead-Sullivan
Explore the repertoire of the "Great American Songbook" with this 70-song collection, masterfully arranged by Alan Munde and Beth Mead-Sullivan for 3-finger, Scruggs-style 5-string banjo. Rhythm tab, right hand fingerings and chord diagrams are included for each of these beloved melodies. Songs include: Ain't She Sweet • Blue Skies • Cheek to Cheek • Home on the Range • Honeysuckle Rose • It Had to Be You • Little Rock Getaway • Over the Rainbow • Sweet Georgia Brown • and more.
00156862 ....$19.99

How to Play the 5-String Banjo
Third Edition
by Pete Seeger
This basic manual for banjo players includes melody line, lyrics and banjo accompaniment and solos notated in standard form and tablature. Chapters cover material such as: a basic strum, the fifth string, hammering on, pulling off, double thumbing, and much more.

14015486 ....$19.99

O Brother, Where Art Thou?
Banjo tab arrangements of 12 bluegrass/folk songs from this Grammy-winning album. Includes: The Big Rock Candy Mountain • Down to the River to Pray • I Am a Man of Constant Sorrow • I Am Weary (Let Me Rest) • I'll Fly Away • In the Jailhouse Now • Keep on the Sunny Side • You Are My Sunshine • and more, plus lyrics and a banjo notation legend.

00699528 Banjo Tablature $17.99

Clawhammer Cookbook
Tools, Techniques & Recipes for Playing Clawhammer Banjo
by Michael Bremer
The goal of this book isn't to tell you how to play tunes or how to play like anyone else. It's to teach you ways to approach, arrange, and personalize any tune – to develop your own unique style. To that end, we'll take in a healthy serving of old-time music and also expand the clawhammer palate to taste a few other musical styles. Includes audio track demos of all the songs and examples to aid in the learning process.
00118354 Book/Online Audio $22.99

The Ultimate Banjo Songbook
A great collection of banjo classics: Alabama Jubilee • Bye Bye Love • Duelin' Banjos • The Entertainer • Foggy Mountain Breakdown • Great Balls of Fire • Lady of Spain • Orange Blossom Special • (Ghost) Riders in the Sky • Rocky Top • San Antonio Rose • Tennessee Waltz • UFO-TOFU • You Are My Sunshine • and more.

00699565 Book/Online Audio $29.99

Visit Hal Leonard online at **www.halleonard.com**

Learn to Play Today
with folk music instruction from Hal Leonard

Hal Leonard Bagpipe Method

The Hal Leonard Bagpipe Method is designed for anyone just learning to play the Great Highland bagpipes. This comprehensive and easy-to-use beginner's guide serves as an introduction to the bagpipe chanter. It includes access to online video lessons with demonstrations of all the examples in the book! Lessons include: the practice chanter, the Great Highland Bagpipe scale, bagpipe notation, proper technique, grace-noting, embellishments, playing and practice tips, traditional tunes, buying a bagpipe, and much more!

00102521 Book/Online Video $16.99

Hal Leonard Banjo Method – Second Edition

Authored by Mac Robertson, Robbie Clement & Will Schmid. This innovative method teaches 5-string, bluegrass style. The method consists of two instruction books and two cross-referenced supplement books that offer the beginner a carefully-paced and interest-keeping approach to the bluegrass style.

00699500 Book 1 Only...$9.99
00695101 Book 1 with Online Audio..............$17.99
00699502 Book 2 Only...$9.99
00696056 Book 2 with Online Audio..............$17.99

Hal Leonard Brazilian Guitar Method

by Carlos Arana

This book uses popular Brazilian songs to teach you the basics of the Brazilian guitar style and technique. Learn to play in the styles of Joao Gilberto, Luiz Bonfá, Baden Powell, Dino Sete Cordas, Joao Basco, and many others! Includes 33 demonstration tracks.

00697415 Book/Online Audio..........................$17.99

Hal Leonard Chinese Pipa Method

by Gao Hong

This easy-to-use book serves as an introduction to the Chinese pipa and its techniques. Lessons include: tuning • Western & Chinese notation basics • left and right hand techniques • positions • tremolo • bending • vibrato and overtones • classical pipa repertoire • popular Chinese folk tunes • and more!

00121398 Book/Online Video $19.99

Hal Leonard Dulcimer Method – Second Edition

by Neal Hellman

A beginning method for the Appalachian dulcimer with a unique new approach to solo melody and chord playing. Includes tuning, modes and many beautiful folk songs all demonstrated on the audio accompaniment. Music and tablature.

00699289 Book...$12.99
00697230 Book/Online Audio..........................$19.99

Hal Leonard Flamenco Guitar Method

by Hugh Burns

Traditional Spanish flamenco song forms and classical pieces are used to teach you the basics of the style and technique in this book. Lessons cover: strumming, picking and percussive techniques • arpeggios • improvisation • fingernail tips • capos • and much more. Includes flamenco history and a glossary.

00697363 Book/Online Audio..........................$17.99

Hal Leonard Irish Bouzouki Method

by Roger Landes

This comprehensive method focuses on teaching the basics of the instrument as well as accompaniment techniques for a variety of Irish song forms. It covers: playing position • tuning • picking & strumming patterns • learning the fretboard • accompaniment styles • double jigs, slip jigs & reels • drones • counterpoint • arpeggios • playing with a capo • traditional Irish songs • and more.

00696348 Book/Online Audio..........................$12.99

Hal Leonard Mandolin Method – Second Edition

Noted mandolinist and teacher Rich Del Grosso has authored this excellent mandolin method that features great playable tunes in several styles (bluegrass, country, folk, blues) in standard music notation and tablature. The audio features play-along duets.

00699296 Book...$10.99
00695102 Book/Online Audio..........................$16.99

Hal Leonard Oud Method

by John Bilezikjian

This book teaches the fundamentals of standard Western music notation in the context of oud playing. It also covers: types of ouds, tuning the oud, playing position, how to string the oud, scales, chords, arpeggios, tremolo technique, studies and exercises, songs and rhythms from Armenia and the Middle East, and 25 audio tracks for demonstration and play along.

00695836 Book/Online Audio..........................$14.99

Hal Leonard Sitar Method

by Josh Feinberg

This beginner's guide serves as an introduction to sitar and its technique, as well as the practice, theory, and history of raga music. Lessons include: tuning • postures • right- and left-hand technique • Indian notation • raga forms; melodic patterns • bending strings • hammer-ons, pull-offs, and slides • changing strings • and more!

00696613 Book/Online Audio..........................$16.99
00198245 Book/Online Media..........................$19.99

Hal Leonard Ukulele Method

by Lil' Rev

This comprehensive and easy-to-use beginner's guide by acclaimed performer and uke master Lil' Rev includes many fun songs of different styles to learn and play. Includes: types of ukuleles, tuning, music reading, melody playing, chords, strumming, scales, tremolo, music notation and tablature, a variety of music styles, ukulele history and much more.

00695847 Book 1 Only...$8.99
00695832 Book 1 with Online Audio..............$12.99
00695948 Book 2 Only...$7.99
00695949 Book 2 with Online Audio..............$11.99

HAL•LEONARD®

Visit Hal Leonard Online at
www.halleonard.com

Prices and availability subject to change without notice.